FIND YOUR

YOU

FIND YOUR

YOU

TONY ASHCRAFT

This book is dedicated to the
Krzeminski family.

FOREWORD

In your day-to-day life, how many people do you come across that seem drained and tired of the daily grind? I am gonna bet it's a lot. Do you find yourself feeling this way, too? Are you happy about how you're living your life? Is Monday your favorite day of the week? If not...know that it doesn't have to be this way.

For most of my life, I felt like I had no control over who I was. I was taught (as most of us are) to listen to my parents and fall in line with the rules of society, without question. I was made to believe my purpose was to join the workforce as soon as I graduated college. Put money in my retirement account. Get married, buy a home, have kids. We all are...

After having my ego shattered into a million pieces, trying to hold up and live up to an image of myself that I just wasn't, I began questioning who I really was, and what I really wanted in this life. As I was searching for meaning and putting all my focus and energy into ME, suddenly, everything changed. For the first time I realized I had pushed down my true nature to be what I thought I should be, rather than the person I truly was. I picked up a pen and paper and started to write about it, and began to unravel the layers of the person I'd created, and of who I really was.

My book, Find Your YOU, is all about how I transitioned my life from the framework of society to finding my authentic self and true purpose, resulting in a life I truly love.

I wanted to set out to create something truly unique – something truly "Me," so I made this book an actionable and unique experience for every reader who joins me on this journey.

You have the power to live your best, most authentic life.

The journey is the greatest gift of the process. Life is a reflection of yourself. What I want for others is how I want my life to be. I applied a few elements to my daily life and to the people around me, and it had a tremendous impact on my own experiences, which enabled me to become a better version of myself. I hope these concepts will do the same for you. They are:

Positive: Sometimes in life, the glass may not be half full, but Find Your YOU aims to help you see that it can be. That even in dark, destructive times, where you feel lost and unsure, there are messages from the universe signaling you on the path to a brighter day.

Compassionate: Find Your YOU was created to help others, based on a deep-rooted sense of caring about the struggles and hardships everyone faces in life. Through my message, I seek to find ways to help, because I can sympathize, and want to see everyone live an authentic, happy life.

Passionate: The message of Find Your YOU is one I have felt energy around for so long. It is a message I have put into practice in my life, and feel incredibly passionate about sharing with others.

Courageous: Fearlessness has been a consistent theme in my life. From leaving jobs, people, and situations that no longer benefitted me, I have faith in myself, and the power of the universe to guide me in the direction I need to go. I encourage you to do the same, and Find Your YOU!

CONTENTS

CONTENTS

CHAPTER ONE

FOLLOWING THE SYSTEM

Luke 12:2 *The time is coming when everything that is covered up will be revealed, and all that is secret will be made known to all.*

The Collective Consciousness

When we are born into this world, we come into a place that is surrounded by peace and love, and everything is in perfect harmony. We are nurtured by our caretakers and fear very little. We subconsciously know that we are safe. We are fed when we need to be fed, we are sheltered when we are cold, and we are held close to the hearts and protected by those who love us. Our environment becomes predictable until it isn't. We soon realize the world we live in is not entirely safe. We become exposed to loud noises and high places, which will be known as our first two fears. From there, our subconscious is conditioned for the next 7 years of our lives and becomes further ingrained in the years to come.

As we grow up, we are continuously conditioned on how to think. We are taught what is good or bad, right or wrong, and, sadly, how we should feel. As children, we are taught what it's like to be "ladylike" or what is considered "manly." We often are confused by new emotions because we have been programmed to think our feelings are wrong if they do not fit the narrative of what society intended for us to believe. We become accustomed to how we shape our views in this world, and it becomes habituated as our standard form of living. As we grow older, this belief system becomes our comfort zone.

Outside of how we view ourselves, we take notice of what is expected from us by society. Humans have one quality that we all share: the need to belong. As we shape our views of ourselves, we feel the need to belong and conform to the system that has been laid before us. Wherever you live in the world, it is made up of systems and structure to govern the global population, and it can vary by culture. The system for America is not the same as the system for an indigenous tribe in Africa, but they are similar because they each provide the balance of structure. Each is given a certain set of rules and laws which we must abide by. Most of these guidelines are in place to protect us so that we may coexist in a society that has been built before us. It becomes so ingrained in our subconscious that it becomes our nature.

Everything we invite into our consciousness becomes planted into our subconscious, which makes up 95% of our reality. The accumulation of these shared thoughts and beliefs is known as the collective consciousness and is the makeup of the physical world in which we live. The collective consciousness is a shared belief system of ideas, which functions as the joining force in our society. What we currently accept in our society has been agreed upon by the collective of our world as a whole. We accept this world the way it is because it's the only reality that is shown to us. If someone were to say something that fell outside the spectrum of our collective consciousness, they might be accused of being "crazy." Most of us become so entangled within our collective consciousness that it becomes hard to break our belief system.

Consciousness means perception. Collective consciousness is not fixed and is always evolving. We are sending and receiving signals as a global consciousness that has become our fixed way of life, until the thought pattern is challenged. For example, there was a belief that it was completely impossible for anyone to run a sub-four-minute mile. It was considered physically impossible to do so. The world collectively shared this belief, which became part of the global collective consciousness. Roger Bannister did not believe this to be true and separated himself from the collective consciousness. On May 6, 1954, he became the first person to run a mile in 3 minutes and 59.4 seconds. He single-handedly broke the belief that it was impossible and shifted the global consciousness to believing that the feat could be done. Because of the shift in collective consciousness, his record held up for 46 days, and suddenly it became common to run a mile in under four minutes. All it took was a shift in consciousness.

Our reality is affected by our beliefs. Even when an individual is able to break free from the collective consciousness the way Roger Bannister did, greater things can be accomplished when there is collectiveness from a group. When people share a common goal, they have the ability to accomplish even greater things, ones that were once believed to be unachievable. Napoleon Hill referred to this as the mastermind group. Henry Ford understood the power of a mastermind group. He hired a group of engineers to put together an eight-cylinder engine. His engineers told him, "It's impossible." After a year had passed, Henry Ford's goal had not been achieved. He ordered his engineers to continue with the discovery. Then, out of nowhere, the secret was found. The power of the mastermind group became the collective consciousness subgroup, focused on a common goal, which allowed them to put something together that had seemed impossible and out of reach. As Henry Ford states, "Whether you think you can or you can't – you're right." In other words, in order for there to be a shift in consciousness, the change must occur from within.

The mind is more powerful than we are led to believe. There have been many examples where the mind has contested the laws of science and physics. There has been footage of a Tibetan monk levitating, cancer and tumors have been removed without medicine, and there are people who always win the lottery. There are forces in this universe that go beyond our comprehension, but oftentimes we find ourselves stuck in a belief system that holds us back from infinite possibilities, keeping us in a system that may not serve us.

What would happen if monks levitating, or tumors and cancer being removed without medical treatment, became mainstream? It would challenge the current belief system in what was possible.

From these examples alone, we see that the mind is extremely powerful and is always expanding the collective consciousness. Your mind has the ability to give you superpower abilities. When you believe something is impossible, and then suddenly you see someone else do it, it now becomes possible. Nothing changed except the belief that it can be done. In order to accomplish what you want, you have to do something you never did. You do not need to wait for someone else to pave the way for you. As Robert Frost said, "Take the road less traveled." When you are able to do something outside the ordinary way of thinking, you are basically uploading new thoughts and beliefs into the cloud of our collective consciousness, contributing to and expanding upon an endless list of global possibilities.

Our collective consciousness is tied to how our society operates, and it affects everything we do today, including the makeup of our entire belief system. We are essentially imprisoned by our beliefs because they become our expectations. Our lives become so systemic and routine that it almost feels like we don't have to think for ourselves. Today's system has become so natural to us that we have grown accustomed to it being our only way of life. The expectations are laid out right in front of us. We are expected to go to school, get good grades, stay out of trouble, graduate, either attend college or trade school or find a job, buy a home, pay our bills, get married, have kids, not break the law, and retire.

In today's world, we are deeply rooted and connected to our current system. The political, educational, social, and economic systems are the primary engines that tie us together, but at the same time the system gives us the illusion that we are separate from each other. Wherever you are from, your community upholds the same morals and values for these systems. You are expected to abide by these standards or face consequences.

When I was young, I always wondered why these structures were in place. Many of these things did not make sense to me. Some parts of the system I loved, and other parts were confusing. I loved going to school so that I could see my friends, learn something new, and be social. I remember when I had to learn about politics for the first time in 3rd grade and had to choose a presidential candidate. This was confusing to me because I felt my parents deserved authority over me since they knew what was best for me, not some elected official. I thought to myself: Why should I care? It did not end there. I also questioned the rituals we had to follow at church, some of the subject matter we had to learn in school, and often hearing "you can't" whenever I wanted to dabble in something new. My questions were always the same: Why? Every time I was pulled into something that felt unnatural, it felt like a part of my spirit was pulled away from me.

When you take a closer look at these systems in place and determine how they really function, do you ever wonder if it's actually working? Do you feel the system is expanding or limiting your potential? Ask yourself, does this system serve you? If not, what can you do to break free from it? If it does serve you, then what can you do to improve it? How can we become better than we already are? Since we have a foundation in place, what can we do so there are not any homeless people in this world? Should mental and emotional health be taught in our schools? The collective consciousness of this world wants you to think there is scarcity in food supply, but this is not the universal truth. There is an abundance of food, enough to feed the entire world, but in 2016, 5.6 million children under the age of 5 died due to hunger. That is 15,000 children a day. What can we do to prevent this from happening? How can we reallocate our resources for the betterment of humanity across the world? Once again, all it takes is a shift in global consciousness that there IS enough to go around.

We have the opportunity to create a world that serves everyone's needs. According to Deepak Chopra and the law of pure potentiality, we can "create anything, anytime, anywhere." As shown in the examples above, it only takes one person to create a shift in our collective consciousness. When something new is created, it then uploads into our cloud of consciousness and becomes our new reality. We have been inundated by people who tell us we can't. What we often fail to realize when someone says something negative is that it is a reflection of them, not you. In other words, when someone says, "You can't," they are telling you their limitations, not yours.

If you have ever found yourself living in fear or being stuck or complacent with life, don't worry. You are not alone. These are ALL learned behaviors that we have picked up from people we associate closely with. This generally begins in our early years, as it is taught by our parents, schoolteachers, and religious instructors. We attempt to discover our true self by imitating others, which inadvertently enforces our limitations. The only difference between limitations and imitations is the letter "L." In sports, an "L" refers to a loss. We learn about these limitations from our imitations of others, which is the makeup of our collective consciousness. Imitation leads to restrictions. These restrictions are then passed on to us by our classmates, celebrities, and what we see on TV, further expanding our collective consciousness as to how the world functions.

Throughout this book, you will see terms being used, such as systems, rules, structure, control, conditioning, programming, etc. as subcategories to our collective consciousness. You will see that when you become aware of your situation, you have the power to create a life you desire, and that it has been within you all along. This book outlines a comprehensive approach that I have learned from over a few dozen new thought authors who have helped me discover my true purpose. I give examples of my life's experiences throughout this book and introduce concepts that I identified with as I was beginning my transformation. You will learn how these key concepts can be applied in your everyday life, enabling you to transform your inner self, becoming who you are destined to be.

When you look within, you will discover there is a secret identity hiding inside you. By unraveling the layers, you have the ability to create a life of abundance, pure joy, and happiness, and it starts by having the right mindset. Believe that what you want has already come into existence, and watch the signs of the universe lay out the path before you. Now let's examine where it all started . . .

The Journey and a Hidden Agenda

I went to school, was expected to get good grades, graduate, went to and completed college, found a career, got married, bought a house. I was making my parents proud of my accomplishments and society even prouder, because I was conforming to its system. There was one problem though: I was not happy.

I felt like the choices I made were controlled by higher entities, trickled down and influenced by propaganda, parents, teachers, friends, social and societal expectations. Taking risks was considered a destructive behavior, so conforming was thought of as the right thing to do, or so I was told. Whenever I felt like resisting, there was even more pressure from what was expected of me in the next stage in my life. During my senior year in college, I did not have any idea what I wanted to do for the rest of my life. However, I was expected to hurry up and make a decision, placing unneeded urgency on choosing something I would stick to until retirement.

After landing a life-changing gig prior to graduating college, which I will discuss in chapter 5, a friend's mother did not congratulate me. Instead, she asked, "When are you going to graduate?" I placed pressure on myself, and also felt pressure from others around me, making me feel I had to urgently comply within the system. For a split second, I thought, "This gig is only temporary, and I need to start preparing for my future." So many people fall victim to what is "expected," and the need to fall in line to what is "right." I knew I had the rest of my life to graduate, but still felt unnecessary urgency to finish school, and anxiety about putting my future on hold.

To be clear, there is no urgency to decide what you should be doing for the next 30 years. You do not need to immediately choose a career. Slow down, enjoy the journey, and watch the process unfold before you. Do what feels right for you, not for your parents, teachers, or other external influences.

People are programmed into thinking that you need to stick to the structure that is already in place, but sadly, they do not always have your best interests at heart. They may not want to see you succeed beyond what they have accomplished. They may downplay your victories from being stepping-stones towards your path to joy, happiness, and fulfillment by creating an illusion that these "temporary" explorations are a disruption towards your destiny, similar to being pebbles in your shoe. They may view these victories as a distraction from the main objective and may plant negative subliminal messages into your mindset, lowering your morale in the process.

Whether you attend college, a trade school, or work right after graduating high school, you are pressured into being a cog in the system rather than following your heart or passion. When you were a kid, you played with what you loved. You had an imagination that could go on forever. As you got older, the expectations of play shrunk down into direction, focus, and conforming. You began to find yourself trapped in a box or psychological prison where it became hard to escape.

What happened to your inner child? Is it still there, needing to come out? Remember when you were younger and able to play every day? Life was fun. Your natural instincts were kicking in. Part of your experience was the discovery of what worked and what did not work through simple experiments and observations. You created an image, which led to a hypothesis. After putting your theory to the test, you made observations on how the experiment either worked or did not. Then you began to modify your experiments in every which way you could, and some worked, and some didn't. When reflecting, you realize that the journey of the experiment was more engaging and entertaining than the result.

As Neil deGrasse Tyson has stated, "Kids are born scientists." Kids' imaginations are infinite. There are endless possibilities, as long as it can be imagined. As we get older, our window of imagination and creativity begins to dwindle as our minds become programmed into structure. Comments from people we respect, such as parents, teachers, siblings, friends, as well as people on media outlets, begin to influence our thoughts, and we believe them.

We are often told things that limit our capabilities, such as, "You're not a scientist," or "Acting is a pipedream. Stick to something more realistic." "Will you stop singing? You sound terrible." This has negative long-term effects on someone's mindset, closing the door to any further advancement.

When someone is speaking about your limitations, they are merely showing a reflection of themselves, not you. Ignore damaging statements, such as, "You have to be smart to do that." "You've never done it before. How are you going to do that?" "I tried it, and it doesn't work." "It's about who you know." "You need a college degree to be successful." When someone is telling you to take action, whether they experienced it themselves or not, they are repeating what they were told. Instead of learning for themselves, they became programmed within the system, and they coexist in society through the ways that they were taught. Many never experience life on their own, and choose the path of working to live rather than living to work.

You may find yourself filling your mind with toxic media news coverage, highlighting all the negativity in the world. As you try to escape from it, you often see posts on social media that encourage the same. During the news coverage, subliminal messages are being planted in your mind from commercials, politicians, celebrities, and other propaganda. This can range from the temptation of alcohol, unhealthy food, how you should conform, or images of someone's wealth in order to keep up with the Joneses. You find yourself becoming inspired about having the perfect body, while you continue to devalue your self-worth. You continue to unknowingly plant toxic thoughts in your head as to what the ideal body or what the ideal life should be, because you are trying to absorb and take in as much information as possible. Unfortunately, you are getting your information from the wrong sources and the trend continues for years until you feel locked in your situation. You start viewing yourself as too fat or too skinny, or the current job or career you have is not entirely what you expected, so you begin to doubt your self-worth because of the life choices you've made.

The majority of the population lacks imagination and creativity, so they follow trends on social media and in the media, whether they are for something or against it. Even when there are two sides, they feel they are making a choice by picking one side of the argument over the other. Most people allow the limitations society has planted to justify complacency in their life. For example, they may place blame on a political party as if it was their fault that they cannot get ahead in life. They will take the path of least resistance, become miserable with their position in life, and accept it because everyone else is doing it, becoming part of the 98%. Napoleon Hill suggests anytime someone simply tolerates an irritating situation, whether it is a job/career, environment, social circle, companion, or anything else, they are a follower – the 98% club. Trust your intuition when the feeling is unnatural.

Unfortunately, people in your environment are not the only ones who will amplify your misery of complacency. Once we reach a certain age, we are in control of who enters and who leaves our life. By the time we get a chance to make these choices, we have already set a pattern in place. Our previous experiences lead to the self-image we have created, listening and believing we are a product of our environment.

Up until this point, you attracted people and a lifestyle based on your thoughts. Your environment is not who you are, it is who you were. You have the ability to respond by removing yourself from a situation you are not compatible with, and create a new life for yourself. Oftentimes people defer to negativity about life being unfair, leading to a downward spiral of despair, thinking it is too late to make a change, but you have complete control in how you respond.

Defeating comments to justify your inabilities such as, "I'm not smart enough to be a doctor," or, "I'll never get that promotion," or, "It's too hard," are all self-defeating comments that cause you to become a follower who is complacent with your life choices. Being negative in the present sounds like a natural path in the moment, but I can assure you, being positive with everything life throws your way will have a tremendous impact. Instead of being disturbed by a negative encounter: ask yourself what is it that can be gained from this experience; what is the universe telling me? Being positive will inevitably be the easiest way to live. You are in control of your emotions and how you respond.

Should You Be a Cog?

Society wants you to be just like everyone else, so you feel obligated to become a cog in the system. This is NOT you! You are an intelligent being with unlimited potential. Have you ever studied for something, read a book, gotten distracted, and had to go back over and reread it again? And even when you go back again, you begin to drift off and lose your focus all over again? Do you feel unmotivated by mundane tasks? This isn't because you are not smart. You are just like everyone else when it comes to this sort of thing. Did you know that the average person loses their attention span for 6-10 seconds every minute? I lose my attention all the time. This is not ADHD. This is being human.

We compare ourselves with classmates or the national average for the grades we score. We are led to believe that these scores represent our intelligence. There are nine types of intelligence. They are:

- Naturalist (nature)
- Musical (sound)
- Logical-mathematical (number/reasoning)
- Existential (life)
- Interpersonal (people)
- Bodily-kinesthetic (body)
- Linguistic (word)
- Intra-personal (self)
- Spatial (picture)

Your grades are not indicative of your intelligence. Someone who scored higher than you might have found more value in the information you were learning, or they were more entertained by the content than you. It does not mean you are less smart. You just did not value the subject matter as much as your friends did, or your homelife might be a distraction so you could not properly focus.

Information is limited. If I have not learned something that I should have learned earlier, I will simply say, "I haven't learned that yet. Can you please explain it to me?" You will find more often than not people are willing to be helpful when explaining the subject matter to you. It also makes them feel good about themselves, because they are now offering a valued service.

When someone is critical of your lack of information, it is a reflection of them, not you. Do not let someone's negative attitude regarding your ignorance dictate your self-esteem. They may appear informed about the subject matter, but you do not know if they Googled the content a day earlier and their personality is what compels them to act superior to you. The more knowledge you have, the more informed you will be. This has little to do with intelligence.

When comparing someone's intelligence, or skill set, 1.23% does not seem like a huge percentage gap. A 95% versus 93% on a test is a small margin. Batting a .350 versus a .338 in baseball is also not a large gap. The DNA difference between a human and a chimpanzee is 1.23%. You would not dare to compare a chimpanzee's intelligence to a human. You wouldn't expect a chimpanzee to run errands, act civil in a classroom or work environment, or drive a car because their intelligence level does not allow them to comply with basic rules, structure, and forward-thinking.

You are capable of learning anything there is to know. You have the components within your brain to learn anything. If you want to learn quantum physics at any age, you are capable of learning it. You are not a chimpanzee. You do not have limitations. The only difference between someone who is "smart" and someone who is less informed is the amount of time spent programming your brain on how to think and what content to learn. Do not compare your intelligence to someone else. Just because they may have learned it before you does not mean you are incapable of learning it as well. We all go through different stages in life and have different experiences and various obstacles to overcome. The gap of being informed versus uninformed is very small.

What Is Success?

Success comes in many different forms and is different from person to person based on perspective. Society wants you to believe that success comes from a cookie-cutter template and to accept things the way they are: graduating from college, job/career, paying bills, getting married, buying a house, having kids, advancing in your career, raising children to be successful like you, having grandchildren, being debt-free, retiring, and reflecting on your accomplishments before entering the next phase of eternal life. That sounds about right. One thing they never ask is: "Are you happy?"

You have the potential to break from what is accepted and open the door to new opportunities based on your beliefs. Do not accept that "this is just the way it is" because nothing will change. It starts with YOU! You will soon discover the power that you have within you. Your emotions, energy, thoughts, and imagination carry a lot of weight as you pave the way for your future self. The power you have within you affects people around you. People will subconsciously feel the vibe you are sending based on how you feel about yourself. You will find people are drawn to you when you are sending positive waves of vibration out into the universe.

The opposite happens when you are addressing negative vibes

as well. When you decide to do harm to yourself, you are affecting those who are attached to you. Whether it is a loved one, parent, sibling, friend, colleague, etc., even when you feel your negativity is only hurting yourself, you are affecting others around you, especially those who genuinely care for you.

Substance Abuse?

Alcohol and substance abuse have been serious problems in the US for many years. Everyone knows someone who is affected by this disease. 80-85% of the population today is either on alcohol or another drug of some kind. 70% of the population is on a prescription drug and 90% of the population is ingesting chemicals, unknowingly, including the food we eat. If you or someone you know has been taken by this disease, there is a healthy way out: by becoming informed and aware of your situation.

Many of us think that because alcohol or prescription drugs have been accepted into our culture, they are a conventional form of celebration or are good for medicinal use. We give up our power and control to higher powers about what is right or wrong, legal and illegal, and medication doctors prescribe or do not prescribe, as if the participating parties are doing what is best for us.

When you give away your power to these entities, you allow yourself to become less informed, which has been accepted in our culture for years. We allow ourselves to be controlled by these governing bodies simply based on the titles they own, which oftentimes conflicts with what is right for us. Listen to your body and your mind will lead to the path of enlightenment, which is a far greater drug than can ever be prescribed.

I used to have high blood pressure. My mother has high blood pressure, so I figured it was hereditary. I initially accepted it as part of my life and had to take a pill to control it. However, instead of accepting it, I reflected back on my life and tried to discover why I have high blood pressure. I asked myself, what had changed that might suddenly cause high blood pressure?

While I was taking medication in an attempt to control my high blood pressure, I was searching inside to remove the cause. A few things in my diet had changed. I was eating more processed foods, drinking a couple beers during the evening, and had been working out less and less, all of which I used as an excuse to keep up with the stressful demands of my teaching position. I used excuses and kept saying to myself, "Once this school year ends, I will get back into my routine." Unfortunately, my new habits took precedence over my old habits.

Attracting Like Energy into Your Subconscious

I noticed the way I was feeling attracted similar occurrences in my life. When I was feeling negative energy within me, I was projecting negativity into the universe. This meant I was attracting more negativity because of the way I thought and felt. The feeling was like being stuck in quicksand and sinking fast. I was making excuses for my current situation instead of taking ownership of it. Not only was I affecting myself, but I was also affecting the people I loved and cared for without ever realizing it. I did not think for one second that the harm I was doing to myself had a destructive impact on those around me.

People oftentimes use negative self-talk as a coping mechanism. This can mean saying things like, "I'm too fat," "I'm lazy," "I'm stupid," "I'll never be flexible enough for yoga," etc. When you send negative messages out into the universe, they develop a life of their own and evolve into something bigger in your subconscious, which will be discussed in greater detail in chapter 3. Your subconscious controls you whether you believe it or not, and it does not know when you are joking or when you are serious. While sending out negative affirmations, you are ultimately sabotaging your life purpose by beating yourself up and planting unwanted seeds into your subconscious.

Even though you see yourself as unaffected by your negative habits, either thought or physical, you are severely affecting yourself and those around you, especially people who genuinely care about you. We have all experienced these toxic behaviors, whether it is personal or from someone we know. You may assume "it won't happen to me" because you feel you are in control of your life regardless of what your subconscious dictates. Your conscious state of mind is an illusion. You are at the mercy of your subconscious mind and it still has control over you.

Good habits take form just as easily as bad habits. It takes 21 days to create a habit, 90 days to make it part of your lifestyle. The new habit will become your lifestyle, and evolve into your subconscious mind, putting the energy in motion. Habits are similar to addiction: poor habits can be stopped; good habits can be started.

Wakeup Calls

People are energy. Like attracts like. You have the power to shift your energy from negative to positive by changing the way you think. As Dr. Wayne Dyer states, "If you change the way you look at things, the things you look at will change." When you do not allow yourself to accept things for the way they are, the change you are seeking will not happen. The universe is always conspiring to work for you. These alerts are like wakeup calls that should never be ignored. Once you start searching for the true meaning of events happening in your life, you will begin to see how the universe is always working for you.

Having high blood pressure was my first wakeup call to my health. It made me reflect on how I was affecting myself mentally and physically. I reestablished a few things in my life from when I was younger – energized and enthused with everything life had to offer. I began by changing my eating habits, exercising daily, quit drinking alcohol, and began focusing on a lifestyle that stimulated personal growth. I changed careers twice in the interim before solely concentrating on things that made me happy.

The result was significant after making a few lifestyle choices. Every day steadily became better than the day before. I no longer had high blood pressure, I began having the focus, clarity, and drive to pursue my passion, and loved making the most out of every day. The energy, motivation, and enthusiasm became similar to the feeling I had after graduating high school. The world was my oyster and I had the entire world ahead of me with unlimited potential. I simply took the advice I would have given to my 20-year-old self.

From where you stand today, you can create a life beyond imagination. As you begin your journey, ask yourself, "What does it mean to exist?" Are you existing simply to make a living? If so, you are locking away your untapped potential until you are ready to wake it up from hibernation. When we are simply existing, we are becoming a cog in the conformist society system.

If you are currently employed, you may have a boss that allows limited freedom of control to choose what you want to do, or assigns mindless, numbing tasks that have to be done to benefit the company. This benefits the company, but it may not benefit you. Your energy is being harnessed into the company when in reality it can be used for yourself. This is not how life is intended to be lived. Start living for you. When you stop trying to be what other people want you to be, it opens a world of freedom you never imagined.

Whether you are about to begin your journey or already waist-deep in your current situation, it is never too late to make a shift in focus. You may experience a sense of disorientation and confusion in the beginning. This is natural, because it is the first time you have taken control of your life as you sever ties with your past life. You have been told what to do your entire life by "mentors," many without direction themselves. As you break free from the feeling of being pulled by the wrist, directed in the next step you should take, you will begin to feel a sense of weightlessness.

Open yourself up to the possibilities that surround you. Messages are being sent to you all the time, far from subliminal. It almost feels like you are being slapped on the back of the head, being directed toward the next step you should take. Always listen to the messages that are being sent by the universe and avoid allowing your stubbornness and pressure from others to shift your focus. Never battle with the external voice in your head, telling you what you should be doing. Instead, listen to your internal voice on what it feels like you should be doing. While pursuing what feels right, you will enjoy what you love for the rest of your life.

CHAPTER TWO

THE GRAVITRON

The Ride of a Lifetime

Have you ever been in a situation where you felt stuck or trapped, and the possibility of getting away seemed practically impossible? This can come from a relationship, a roommate situation, or even a job. You might find yourself breaking free from the situation only to find yourself jumping back into something similar, repeating the same patterns and behaviors over and over and again, similar to *Groundhog Day*. These behaviors that make us feel imprisoned by our situation are similar to jumping on a Gravitron, the carnival ride that spins around really fast, exacerbating a gravitational pull over and over again.

Most of us are familiar with the well-known ride at the carnival called the Gravitron. If you are not familiar with the ride, it spins around in circles really fast, raises and tilts, virtually paralyzing you from any sort of movement for approximately 80 seconds. You might be able to move an arm or a leg, maybe lift your head slightly off the mat. But, ultimately, you are not going to be moving anywhere. When the ride stops, you become disoriented and dizzy, feel glad that the ride is over, maybe get sick, but regain your balance and co-ordination and move on to the next ride. Your tolerance determines how long you could stay on the ride. But the ride isn't much different from an undesirable job or living situation. When you sit back and allow it to enter your life, you will see many occasions in your life are similar to jumping on the Gravitron, frozen against your will!

An unpleasant job is similar to being on the Gravitron; it just moves slower. You are on the ride for eight hours a day, five days a week, paralyzed against your freedom, controlled by your situation. Your energy is consumed by this entity for 40 hours a week, not counting commute time. By the end of the week, you feel physically and emotionally drained as if you just got off the Gravitron. After getting off the "ride," you may choose to have a quiet weekend, alone with your family and thoughts, or to celebrate the week by spending your Fridays and weekends unwinding at a local bar/restaurant, catching a football game, or going to the movies. In either scenario, we find ourselves trying to not think about work, only to dread going back to work on Monday.

If this sounds like you, you may want to consider an alternative ride. If you are working a job with no particular aim or purpose that you do not enjoy, you are stuck on the Gravitron. You are simply tolerating a job where your only goal is to make a living. 98% of the population happen to fall victim to making a living instead of living a full and worthwhile life.

Being caught on the Gravitron is not shocking. It has happened to all of us from time to time. As a child, we are highly influenceable. Oftentimes, we need these experiences of being stuck on the Gravitron, so we know precisely what to avoid. Throughout our childhood, we are like sponges, absorbing and processing information in our environment. We are influenced from birth by following the habits and routines from our parents, religious instructors, schoolteachers, family, friends, coworkers, etc., mimicking appealing behaviors. The learned behavior becomes a part of our personalities. We are continuously influenced by media outlets, societal "norms," and all other forms of propaganda to sway us towards their agenda. We have been susceptible to becoming brainwashed in regards to what we should be doing with our lives. Instead, you should be discovering your purpose, uncovering what your true potential can be.

By the time you graduate high school, you have undoubtedly been overwhelmed by a number of influencers attempting to orchestrate the path that you should take in life. You receive direction through their experiences, not yours. It can be from misinformation, propaganda, or possibly from others trying to live through you. Whatever the case may be, you are in control of you. Others may have good intentions for you, trying to become a good mentor or role model, but they are limited by their experiences. If it is from an employer or boss, you might be a piece to their scheme, and they may seek to live out their purpose through you. Ask yourself: what is their agenda, and does it serve your purpose?

We have been inadvertently stuck on the Gravitron of life because it is all we know. These systems are currently in place for you, controlled by your routine. Oftentimes, you do not even realize it, but the habits you have developed since birth become your lifestyle, which currently defines who you are. Your brain has been hardwired since birth, and it is difficult to change who you are. The longer you follow, the more imprisoned you become with your new self and identity. Anyone who does not recognize they have been serving someone else's agenda could be lost in life and never connect with their true potential and discover who they really are.

Are You Stuck on the Gravitron?

How do you know when you are stuck on the Gravitron? Ask yourself, does it feel natural? If you feel like you are being pulled by the wrist and directed where to go, followed by a sense of anxiety, then chances are it is not natural. If the anxiety is interlaced with curiosity and excitement, then enjoy the journey. The decisions you make should come with joy and excitement. If the decision was made by someone else and feels unnatural, you are caught on the Gravitron. You can openly accept advice from others, and you will know right away if the information is good or bad for you. You need to trust your intuition when accepting life choices from others. Be careful whose advice you accept, because you could still be serving someone else's agenda without even realizing it.

People have a difficult time finding their true calling when their daily habits and routines come from being on the Gravitron. Instead, complacency leads to being stuck. This happens in all aspects of life, not just from a job. These patterns continue into your relationships, financial matters, health and nutrition, and all other areas of your life. You become accustomed to these habits because it has been your routine. The sooner you become aware of your habits, the quicker you can break them.

People's habits become expectations from others. Those who remain in the same environment, around the same family and friends, may find it difficult to break free from their habits. When you try to change something about yourself, whether you want to quit drinking, take on a new job, or start eating better, you may be bothered by having to explain the sudden "change" in your behavior to those who know the "old" you. Many prefer to stay imprisoned in the persona they created for themselves in order to avoid uncomfortable conversations.

You are in control of your mind, thoughts, and behavioral patterns. Your habits are only hard to break because you are telling yourself they are hard to break. Do not concern yourself with what others think. This is your life. Start living your life for you, not them.

Break Outside Your Comfort Zone

You may be afraid or find it difficult to break outside your comfort zone because it requires change. This can range from being at the same job, how your family and friends view you, to personal relationships. We often stick to familiarity because it is what we know, and it is what's most comfortable. Instead of making a change, we choose to live in fear of failure and scrutiny. We avoid certain tasks or taking risks and would rather assume our current situation will magically get better without making any real changes. Fear is a mindset. When you live in fear, you are running from something that is not chasing you.

Relationships can be a place of comfort and complacency. A person will only stay in a relationship with someone who treats them a little bit better than they treat themselves. If someone is not entirely happy with the person they are with, they may continue to make compromises in order for the relationship to last, sacrificing their happiness in the process. People will generally tolerate annoying habits for a long time before it really starts to bother them. They choose to stay in the relationship because being without the other person requires change, which makes the person feel uneasy about themselves. Therefore, they continue to stick it out with their partner, hoping their partner will change.

As months go by, their family and friends become accustomed to their partner, so they decide to stay in the relationship even longer. It becomes more difficult to break off the relationship because their family loves the person they are with, and they love the family they belong to. Severing ties would end everything that has brought comfort and joy.

The longer people stay in a struggling relationship, the more compromises people seem to make. The concessions could be superficial, such as they have a decent job, do not do drugs, respect them and their family, are a good person to be around, etc. Therefore, they become afraid to break things off in the relationship because they are worried about how both families will perceive them for ending a relationship that appeared to be so good. So instead of breaking things off, they continue to live with the circumstances of imprisonment. This pattern will continue on and on because they are allowing it to happen.

The only reason they are still in the relationship is because it was easier to stay in the relationship than ending it. When people decide they are okay with being complacent, they are disabling their ability to evolve. When a person decides they deserve better, they will begin to treat themselves better. When something does not feel right, trust your intuition and remove yourself from the situation.

Nothing in your life will improve without you making the changes yourself. As the law of compensation indicates, what you put out into the universe, you will get back. You are not going to see a difference in your situation until you make a change in your lifestyle, inevitably by changing your habits. If your habits are sitting on the couch and watching your favorite television shows every night, you cannot expect a change to happen.

To summarize, end a relationship sooner rather than later if there is not a chance for connectivity and mutual growth. It may be one of the hardest things to do at the time, but it will clearly be the best-case scenario. You no longer need to play a role and continue down the path you do not feel restful with. Stop living in fear of change, and make the changes necessary for you!

Being Trapped in the System

Less than 5% of the population are financially independent. Most live in fear, such as fear of poverty, which is the main reason why 95% of the population is financially dependent. Because of this fear, people avoid taking risks. With this mindset, many decide to live paycheck to paycheck, working a job to earn a living versus living for themselves.

While many are advancing in their careers, they may find themselves staying on the Gravitron, making small concessions along the way. This can range from accepting a small raise, liking the hours, to enjoying the people they work with. Like everything else, what seemed important at the time passed and eventually they find themselves stuck on an island of insignificance, reflecting on their past, wondering where their life has gone.

As people come and go, the working conditions begin to deteriorate their minds. Employees begin to feel trapped in a job without realizing it until it appears to be too late. An employer may attempt to glamorize their employees with small promotions here and there, subtly improving the work environment, and giving extra paid time off in order to keep their employees from leaving. Employees become seduced by their employer's methods for keeping them which soon become expectations and entitlements. An employee might have a glimmer of hope, or an awakening of some kind, and realize these gimmicks are no longer as significant as they once were.

Imagine being surrounded by four walls. As you bounce from one side of the wall to the next, you reach a higher level each time. You become inspired by how high you have climbed the wall, so you share this excitement with your family and friends. We have all been there before. Unfortunately, we don't realize that we are still trapped in the same system. Just because you have reached a higher pedestal in your position does not mean you have elevated your personal growth and development. In fact, growing higher within your position could have quite the opposite effect. Your spirit has been absorbed by this entity that does not have your best interest at heart, and your job becomes a part of your being.

You have already invested so much time, effort, and energy into your job that making a change seems irresponsible and should be the last thing on your mind. Aside from your success, you find you are afraid to leave your job because your family, friends, and acquaintances view you as successful. They see that you have a job with benefits and a retirement plan while making a decent living. As you feed off of their encouragement, you say to yourself you would be a fool if you quit, so you allow this career to define your success story. All this time, while you are considered successful, no one asks if you are happy.

Oftentimes, we become so concerned about appearance, such as labels and job titles and what a job provides, that we stop searching for our identity, and instead buy material things to satisfy our void. We find ourselves attempting to show our success by going on lavish trips, buying expensive cars, living outside our means while racking up more and more debt. The more we try to appear successful on the outside, the more we find ourselves in debt.

We end up spending money we do not have only to make claims that our next pay raise will provide enough financial stability to live the life we desire. However, once the pay raise occurs, we quickly discover it was not enough income to get out of the hole we've put ourselves in. This financial spiral continues because it becomes planted into our subconscious that our expectations are higher than the actual pay raise itself, and we still live in the mindset of there not being enough. We end up chasing our tail in search of financial stability within our job. Without realizing it, we have been sacrificing who we are and what we should be doing to be happy for a job that does not give enough financial security or breathing room to leave the job in the first place. This inevitably causes us to lose touch with our inner self and true purpose.

Your job is what you do and does not define who you are. If you are not happy with your current employment situation, and Monday is not your favorite day of the week, then make a change. Jobs are a dime a dozen. Your talents and skillset far exceed what your employer is looking for, but they may act as if you are easily replaceable to make you feel inadequate regarding your competence. Your feeling of inadequacy will enable your employer to retain you longer and push you to strive for more than your job description requires.

Your résumé already speaks volumes to who you are and what your capabilities can be. Unless your job requires a specific trade, any job can be learned in the field. If you do not feel you are getting the same value of compensation for what you are giving, break free from your current situation and explore new opportunities. Reshape your mold, gain new experiences, meet new colleagues, learn a new trade, and expand your field of consciousness because you never know who will enter your life and what opportunities will evolve from it.

Jobs Create Experience

Take on as many life experiences as you can as often as possible. You can do so by challenging yourself by taking on a new job or a higher position to gain new experiences or perspectives. Every experience has its advantages, as long as you see it as such. The more experiences you have, the more you will be able to differentiate the good from the bad.

Do not concern yourself with what others think when you are bouncing around from job to job. This is perfectly fine. You do not need validation from anyone. Avoid the main problem: taking on a position where you are no longer growing or gaining value. When you feel you have absorbed all of your resources, it is time to move on. This could be from any job. Whether you are a website developer, food and beverage employee, or retail, changing positions can be the ticket to advancing in your life. If you stay with the same mundane job, and are not happy, you will be stuck on the Gravitron and your life will not feel fulfilled.

There is a lot of value to be gained with moving from one job to another. You get to learn how the business operates, analyze their system, and evaluate the overall situation. Learn: What makes them successful? What makes them fail? What could they do to improve the quality of the working conditions? What could they have done so you wouldn't want to leave?

Take an overall assessment of each variable from each company, and you will gain a broader perspective and a wealth of knowledge as you progress in life. It will become something that can be leveraged later. You will know when your time has expired with your company. If now is your time, have a sound backup plan in place, and jump off the Gravitron and gain a new experience.

Changing Your Habits

You have to choose a path when choosing your destiny. The path you take today will become a building block for the trend you are wishing to follow. The more consecutive days your habits exist, the more permanent your habits become. Your habits are contagious, and it affects the pattern you set for your life. It not only affects yourself, but it also attracts similar people into your life. Their habits are equally as contagious as yours. As your habits are affecting those around you, their habits are reverberating back onto you. As Wayne Dyer states, "You don't attract what you want. You attract what you are." If you are not happy with your situation, it is up to you to make a change.

If you want to attract positive people in your life, start today by being more positive. Do not surround yourself with people who always complain and act like the victim. When the people in your social circle experience everything as "doom and gloom" and only report events that are negative, then you are limiting your growth potential. If you find yourself engaging in a conversation where negativity is common, start by being more positive in the conversation, or remove yourself entirely from the conversation, person, or group.

In order to change your situation, change your habits. Focus on one character flaw at a time, something you wish to change about yourself. Start making small steps each day to improve your situation. Become conscientious about your decisions, especially for the first 21 days. If you want to improve your diet and nutritional habits, focus on eating healthy for 21 consecutive days. If you want to get back in shape, do not overstress yourself by trying to get back into shape all at once. Take baby steps each day. Start by walking 2-3 times a week just to get in the habit of healthy living, and eventually scale up to walking more often and increase your activity from there.

Not only are you training your body, but you are also training your mind. If you want to have a healthy mind, create a healthy environment. Surround yourself with positive people. Turn off all the gossip channels and feed your mind with literature and media content that brings you value. Begin feeding your mind with information, even if it is for 30 minutes more today than it was yesterday. Stay humble as you improve your situation. You had a long path to get where you came from, so forgive those who are not aware yet. You do not need to be any better than anyone. Simply focus on being a better person today than you were yesterday.

The goal is to remove yourself completely from the Gravitron of life. When you reflect back on your life, remember why you are the way you are. Try and dig deep into your childhood about what you were taught at a young age that carried over with you into adulthood. You have been programmed to think a certain way since birth. The more you understand why you think the way you do, the quicker you will be able to reprogram your brain on how to think moving forward. You will begin to have awakening experiences. Some awakening moments will be fast and sudden, where other experiences will be similar to having an epiphany like an "ah-ha" moment. It is like your brain is wired into a bunch of knots, slowly unraveling as you begin to experience life for YOU, not others.

Jumping Off the Gravitron

When you take a step back and watch how the world operates, you will begin to see that everything is in sync as you separate yourself from the Gravitron. The flow and rhythm of people's habits do not change. It becomes a programmed, systematic routine of behaviors. When you start to see the big picture of life, your world slows down around you, and your intuition levels increase. You will realize your energy is no longer being sucked from within, and now you can start focusing your newfound energy on yourself.

From your new perspective, you can see the Gravitron spinning around really fast. The difference is that you can open the door, walk in, and watch the world spin and operate all around you without having to be engaged in it. It is the energy in motion. You will not be fazed by the spinning of the ride, but will understand its predictable nature. It will be an awakening moment. You will be able to walk straight through the Gravitron without it pulling you in. It is like your path is laid out for you, and all you have to do is start taking action towards your purpose. Your intuitive nature will become stronger over time, as you can now predict human behavior.

As you become less fazed by external distractions, you start to feel drawn towards a true purpose. You will feel pulled in the direction to receive. As you shield off the distractions that had been absorbing your internal energy, you begin progressing towards your purpose. You will create this vision with conviction and intent and will focus on it until your destination is reached.

The Gravitron is, in a sense, as if you are being controlled. You may experience confusion or anxiety. It often feels like a tug of war with one side pulling you one direction, and on the other side, you trying to pull yourself in your desired direction. You may have felt misdirected, manipulated, or deceived by someone else's agenda. When you become free from the Gravitron, you will feel like you have regained control of your life. If you haven't found it already, then it is time to discover your real purpose. Every day you are free from the Gravitron you take another step closer to discovering oneself. You will feel like you have broken out of the psychological prison that was created before you, and you will start gravitating toward your identity.

Begin to questioning EVERYTHING! Question the people you have in your life. Question the job you have. The haircut. Everything. Remove yourself from the environment to eliminate expectations of yourself, and observe how fast you gravitate towards your purpose. As you are solidly focused on your true purpose, you cannot be fazed by distractions; you will expect them. Now you will know how to respond. You do not have control over what happens in your life, but you have 100% control over how you respond. You can sit back and ask the universe why this particular message is being sent to you, and the answers will begin to line up. As each day feels like a miracle, you will find inner peace with yourself because you took back what is yours: YOUR LIFE!

CHAPTER THREE

THE SUBCONSCIOUS MIND

Ego and the Subconscious

We each have developed a role in society. The developmental stages of our youth become the character we portray. This character becomes who we identify with. Who we identify with is our ego, which will be discussed at greater length in chapter 6. Your YOU has been buried inside of your ego this entire time. You came into this world with the highest form of frequency known as Love. Love yourself first! If you do not love yourself, how do you expect others to love you? You cannot give something you do not have. Give yourself the expression of love first, and then you will be able to give and receive love.

Anything you say has an impact on your life. Your subconscious does not know when you are joking or telling the truth, so it is necessary to speak positively. Self-talk can either be expressed aloud or internally and can have a profound impact. When you are saying negative things such as, "I am stupid," or "I am ugly," or "I am not good enough," you will begin to feel a sense of unworthiness. The same can happen when you are sending out negative messages to other people. Your words have a strong impact and can affect those who you say them to, including yourself.

When you are saying positive things about yourself, such as "I am happy," or "I am successful," or "I am motivated," or "I am good enough," or "I am spiritually connected," you are confirming your intentions to the universe. When you continue to send positive messages to yourself and others around you, you will attract more positivity in your life. To raise your frequency and vibration, practice every morning by saying something positive about yourself. Your affirmations are the effect of your current life's situation.

When you say "I am," you are sending affirmations to the universe, which become absorbed into your subconscious. How you feel about yourself will be the result of your affirmations. Say what you want to experience aloud to create a contract with yourself and the universe that will be hard to break. It is easy to keep secrets to yourself and not follow through, because no one will hold you accountable. Make the agreement with the universe and let it hold you accountable.

The Power Within You

The power of your subconscious mind is limited to what you accept it to be. It controls 95% of your behaviors, thought habits, current situations, and the people in your life. It can attract more wealth, better health, and more joy and happiness when your subconscious mind is programmed properly. In retrospect, the opposite occurs when your habits are controlled with negative thoughts and emotions. Your subconscious is recording every element you invite into your life on an ongoing basis. Whether it be love, faith, desire, happiness, joy, fear, misery, envy, anger, or greed, they become an integral part of your development.

Over 98% of the population is easily influenced by things they see on social media, television, and the movies they watch. Your subconscious does not know the difference between what is fake or real. Oftentimes, people make brash statements about themselves such as, "I am not smart enough. I am not good at that. I will never be good at this." These negative affirmations will be fulfilled, even if you are joking. Be conscious of what you are saying about yourself. Your subconscious mind is recording EVERYTHING. When you are making bold statements about yourself, ALWAYS end your statements with a positive. Replace "I can't" with "I CAN" and you will experience the world in an entirely different new light.

Your reactions, impulses, and instincts are emotions fundamentally driven by the seeds that have been sowed in your subconscious mind through years of repeated habits, transforming you into the person you are today. The people you are surrounded with are a reflection of who you are. It is easy to say that some people are in your life simply by circumstance, though it may be true when you are in your youth living through your parents' agenda. Otherwise, people you work with, friends of friends, social gatherings, etc., are a reflection of who you are.

If you are not willing to make a change, then nothing will actually change; miracles do not happen by blind luck. The average person has 60,000 thoughts per day, and 90% of those thoughts are the same as the day before. Most people are consciously unaware and highly suggestible to their surroundings, which reinforces their position. If you find yourself stuck in a cycle as though you are trapped on the Gravitron, then likely you are.

Your current situation has been predetermined for years by repeat thought habits. Whether it be positive or negative, you have no one to blame for your situation once you realize you are in control of your thoughts. Breaking free from the Gravitron can cause a huge jolt to your frequency and vibration. You may feel some disorientation or confusion at first, but the actual harm you are doing to yourself by remaining in a toxic situation, whether it be from a job, friends, and even family, can be detrimental to your YOU.

YOU Are YOUR Creator

Whether you believe there is or is not a God, you still have faith. Your faith resides in whether God exists or not. You are a creation from God, who lives within you. Being a child of God means you are also God and the creator of your universe. No one is in control of you, except yourself. You are in control of your thoughts, your actions (habits), and emotions. Your thoughts, awareness, actions, and affirmations control your destiny. The path you are on today is the destiny of your future. You have the ability to change your pattern. Oftentimes, people will wait for God to perform miracles. The miracles have to be performed by you, through your vibrations. You create the miracles. Create action, and watch the miracles happen.

Begin your journey to reach your dreams today. Tomorrow is not an option, since tomorrow may never come, therefore tomorrow does not exist. While you are pursuing your dream, you are going to come across many obstacles you must learn to pivot around. These are not setbacks, but points of growth. You cannot grow without learning something new. The mistakes you make today will not be the same mistakes you will make a year or five years from now. There is a process you must access in order to manifest your dreams. Oftentimes, people are living with negative emotions; the most negative of all emotions is fear. Fear of the unknown. Fear of failure. Fear of ill health. Fear of poverty. When fear lives in your mind, it will manifest in your reality. Instead of living with negative emotions, think more positively. Do not look at failure as a blow to your ego, since your ego does not exist either; your ego is self-created. Look at it as a chance to grow and acquire new experiences.

Positive thinking leads to a happy and fulfilling life. You do not have to wait until you have achieved your dreams to be happy. Enjoy the moments while you can, and embrace the little gifts life has to offer. Once you reach your dream, you will look back and wish you had enjoyed the journey even longer. Your dreams are inevitable and will manifest as long as you visualize yourself already in possession of them and take the necessary actions to achieve them.

Each step of the journey is temporary. The journey is when you get to experience the most growth in your life. You will learn who your true friends and family are and who you can trust. This process is the most important because it will help you to remove toxic people and find partnerships you can build an empire with. Being an "overnight success" eliminates the maturation process. Not having a foundation in place will limit your potential to flourish. People are going to come from all angles, but the process will help you become more effective at identifying who you can trust.

If you do not like the path you are on, then it is never too late to shift gears. You have the power to create a new image for yourself. Be mindful of the content you are consuming, and remove content from your life that can be harmful to your self-image and subconscious. Create a new image of yourself. Whoever you want to become, you can choose that image and become it.

You are given a choice every time you reach a new door. You can either walk through the door and see where it leads, or you can leave it closed. You choose which door to walk through based on where you are in your life. You already know the path you took to get to where you are today. The choices you make dictate the path towards your destiny. Take the path your future YOU will be thankful for.

Family Matters?

If you are in a hostile family situation, you do not owe it to them to remain in their life simply because they are "family." Family should not treat other family members with lack of respect and dignity simply because they are the authoritarian in the group. Your subconscious is highly influenced by your environment. If certain family members are predominantly negative, it is up to you to lead by example by having a positive outlook on life. People cannot change unless they are willing to make the changes themselves. All you can do is show them the light. Once you have done everything you can possibly do, if it is still not working, then quietly and independently separate yourself from the group without causing a disturbance. Your reaction will always be a reflection of who you are. If you engage negative with negative, it will only drive the emotion of negativity further.

Try and understand that bitterness and resentment will lead to further animosity in your life. The way a family member has been programmed to think is the result of how they were raised and treated by their parents, friends, and colleagues. As they continued to attract more and more negative emotions, it became an accepted form of behavior to deal with an unfortunate circumstance in a victim-like mentality. The negative form of emotion was seeded deep in their subconscious, which became a habitual way of thinking. It is important to be forgiving of another's behavior, as they know not what they do, it is simply reactionary.

Planting Seeds in a Garden

Any significant change in your life, such as the loss of a job or loved one, moving to a new state, or a catastrophic loss, can lead to a better sense of awareness. As these significant changes take place, you will realize that the ego that you have been building up for all these years will cease to matter anymore. The further you separate yourself from your ego, the more you will be able to penetrate your subconscious mind. Your subconscious mind can easily be reprogrammed the same way it was originally programmed, which is through repetitive thoughts and positive affirmations. If you want to see better health, an abundance of wealth, love, or any other personal goals, you can reprogram your thought habits with positive affirmations.

You can reprogram your subconscious mind as easily as planting seeds in a garden. Your brain is like a sponge and absorbs everything you come into contact with. By feeding your conscious with positive affirmations, you will change your subconscious mind. There are 7 principles you can do every day to reprogram your subconscious mind:

1) **Meditate.** Listen to guided meditations every day, ideally once in the morning and again right before you go to bed. Your subconscious is the most influential at night, so make sure you are providing your mind with the proper thoughts prior to sleeping.

2) **List three things you are grateful for every day.** By listing three things you are grateful for daily for 21 days, you will rewire your brain into being happy.

3) **Turn off the noise.** Anything that is a distraction from achieving your purpose needs to be removed from your life. Turn off the television and replace it with things that serve your desires best.

4) **Find people who will encourage growth.** You are the average of those you associate with. Remove negative people that do not serve you. The right people will raise your frequency and vibration towards greatness.

5) **Look for the silver lining.** If something does not go your way, or the universe is sending you a message that does not seem to fit your needs in the moment, ask yourself what can be gained by this experience. The universe is conspiring to work for you, not against you. Become grateful for the experience as it was a necessary detour to guide you down the right path.

6) **Intention.** Every plan you apply must have definite intention towards your objective. Ask yourself what you expect to get from the plan with every decision you make. If your intentions do not serve your purpose, reevaluate your plan.

7) **Nutrition.** Eat fresh fruits and vegetables to become more connected with your surroundings. Avoid processed foods as much as possible. Over time, you will no longer have the urge or cravings to eat the comfort foods you once enjoyed, as you become more connected with yourself. You will enjoy the foods that feed your body with energy and provide clarity for your mind.

By sticking to these 7 principles, you will reseed your path towards your purpose. As you continue to gain momentum, you will discover new ways that your higher-self will speak to you.

CHAPTER FOUR

SIGNS FROM THE UNIVERSE

The universe is always communicating with you. It is either communicating with you in physical form or being presented on the subconscious level. There are connections, from your thoughts and actions to direct messages being sent. You might say to yourself, "That's a coincidence." There are no coincidences. It is not a coincidence that you are reading this book. You may be trying to sort a few things with your personal or professional life, and this book may be the key that you were looking for.

We are energy transformed into human form. Energy cannot be created or destroyed, and whatever frequency and vibration you send out to the universe will come back to you in another form. You may not be prepared for the messages being sent by the universe, but how you respond is entirely up to you.

There are various ways that messages from the universe are being sent. Ultimately, these messages are coming from your higher self, taking either physical shape or spiritual form. You have the power to tune into your higher self and decipher the messages being shown to you. These messages will not always be as clear as you would like, but when you see one event unfold after another, lining up before you in perfect harmony, you will realize that the universe has been communicating with you all along.

There are several ways the universe is communicating with you and it is up to you to document the messages being sent. Start by recording a journal of your dreams and analyzing what they mean. Record them immediately when you wake up, or they may be lost forever. Your dreams can symbolize events that have been building in your subconscious for a long time. This can range from how you feel about yourself to battles you are struggling with, and can also lead to communication with the divine. Events can play out in your dreams as a premonition from an experience that has not happened yet, giving you the benefit of playing out the situation before it happens. If the dream made you feel uncomfortable, perhaps if you got in a fight with a loved one or sibling, you may wake up and say to yourself, "Thank God it was only a dream." However, the dream was a premonition of your current trajectory playing out. Seeing the events unfold before you might make you realize the future you just experienced is not how you want it to play out. As a result, you can make the decision that you are going to be living a better life and treat the ones you fought with much better, even if they are the ones picking the battles, since it is only a reflection of them. Seeing how your reality plays out demonstrates that you have control of your path by simply changing your frequency. By gaining access to your future self, you have the control to make the right choices before events transpire. You are in control of your destiny.

While you are recognizing your dreams as a means of communication from your subconscious mind, there are a few things to consider when writing them in your daily journal. Remember, dreams are a projection of your subconscious. It does not mean that is how the events will unfold. Use the dream to tap into your emotions. How did the dream make you feel? Were you happy, sad, excited, confused? Next, do a little research on what the dream represents. Was there symbolism involved (falling, losing teeth, being chased, etc.)? You are the expert of your own dreams, so it is up to you to give them meaning. Take all messages into consideration, and if it still does not make sense, leave it for what it is: a dream.

The Universe Aligning You with the Right People

You will attract people based on how you are feeling. When you are having a bad day, or having negative thoughts, you invite the same reality to come into your existence. It might come from someone at the grocery store who is rude, or being cut off on the highway. When this happens, take a step back and reflect on why you are attracting negativity. Do not allow yourself to become aggravated when someone is rude to you. Be aware that your thoughts are like a magnet, and you attract what you think. Their behavior is a reflection of themselves. In order to bring positive people in your life, you must have positive thoughts. When you are positive, you attract positive people.

Most people feel they need to control their situation instead of letting life happen, and tend to ignore the messages that are being sent from the universe in the process. The same pattern exists in relationships. Oftentimes, people live in fear of change and of the unknown. Many will stay at the same job in order to stay inside their comfort zone. Many decide to stay in relationships with friends and companions due to the familiarity of the situation. These relationships would cease to exist if people surrounded themselves with someone compatible. They may fear that if they did not have each other, they would not have anyone in their life. Robin Williams once said, "I used to think the worst thing in life was to end up all alone. It's not. The worst thing in life is to end up with people that make you feel all alone." This is what it feels like when you are with someone incompatible.

Society has placed the burden on most of us to think we need to hurry and find love instead of letting love come to us. This only makes the problem worse, which is why 50% of all marriages end in divorce. People often choose to ignore the inadequacies in their relationships, and bargain with themselves that the relationship can work. Inevitably, it becomes difficult for people to change if they are not willing to make any changes themselves. People can change, but likely not on your terms.

Not Bad People, Just Not Right for You

In a long, committed relationship, you may experience several revealing signs that you and your partner should not be together. However, for the sake of the time spent together, you decide to stick it out for as long as you can, hoping it will work out. As you compromise your well-being, you begin to rationalize the amount of time invested together, thinking that over time your partner will become the person you desire them to be. As time goes by, nothing changes, but you still decide to stay in the relationship.

Being in a bad relationship is like creating a social prison for yourself. You subconsciously have determined that the relationship will not work, but you have become so stubborn and trapped in your ego that you end up ignoring all the signs the universe is sending. This gives you the feeling of a lack of control, as you once again find yourself trapped on the Gravitron without an exit strategy. Sticking with an unhappy relationship is like sticking to a job that you are tolerating because it is what you know; your comfort zone, not your happy zone. Instead of removing yourself from the situation, you find yourself trapped in the world you created.

You may make compromises with your current relationship, the same way you may make compromises with your job. You might try to ignite a spark in the relationship in order to find common ground, so you attempt to travel more, go on dates, or watch the same shows, even though you do not have anything in common. After being together for a long period of time, you become even more aware that you do not have very much in common. You may prefer to go to the gym and focus on your mental and physical health, while your partner likes to hang out with friends and gossip. You might have the desire to live a healthy lifestyle, where your partner wants to eat out every day and have a few drinks with every meal. You might like to sit back and watch a show, where your partner has the desire to build something in the garage. You might have the desire to build a business, where your partner would prefer to stay within their comfort zone with the 9-5 daily grind. You want kids, but your partner does not. You want to live in the city, but your partner wants to live in the suburbs. You prefer the stability of the 9-5, and your partner prefers freelance. While you are experiencing these shortcomings, you may develop a sense of anxiety as the relationship no longer feels right. You begin to feel like you are being pulled from your own life's purpose for the sake of the relationship. As the Gravitron picks up momentum, you start to feel more overwhelmed, even trapped.

Signs from the universe can come at all angles and the discrepancies in your nature reflect who your YOU is. Whichever side of the spectrum you are on is fine, but you should not stay in the relationship if it does not feel right. You should also avoid a relationship if you are not receiving support equal to what you are giving.

It is impossible to multitask. While you are trying to focus on yourself, the distractions from the relationship cause you to lose sight of your purpose and desire. You have removed your YOU to accommodate your relationship. When it feels like your partner is taking you away from achieving your purpose, you have lost sight of the original intent of being in a relationship in the first place. When you are no longer working together towards a common goal, the relationships inevitably defeat the purpose of togetherness. As you notice more situations where you have less and less in common, you become more distant.

When you are in a relationship and it feels like it is preventing you from doing what you prefer to do, then you are making compromises by staying in the relationship. Any sense of tolerance you are experiencing can be avoided by being with the right partner. Sooner rather than later, you become absorbed and anxious by what your partner is doing when you are not together. This distraction pulls you away from focusing on yourself. You soon realize you are drifting apart from your partner, feeling more like roommates. Eventually, the relationship fades as it becomes impossible to ignore how much you have drifted apart. The relationship should have ended much earlier, and the signs from the universe suggest the same. When a situation does not feel right, trust your instincts and listen to your inner voice. It will guide you as long as you are willing to listen.

Many choose to stay in the relationship to protect their ego. You may also stay together for the wrong reasons – your parents really like them; they have a great profession; you are getting older; etc. However, you have a lot less in common than you thought at first glance. What attracted you in the beginning is no longer there or no longer has the same meaning it once did. When these signs do not line up with your goals, you are allowing your ego to get in the way of your desires. When you become aware of your ego, your ego will cease to exist. As Gandhi said, "When the ego dies, the soul awakens." When you stop protecting something that does not exist, you will remember who you are and what you are meant to become.

There Is a Reason for Everything

Imagine where you would be if you received all of your desires without putting forth effort. Would you feel satisfied? Fulfilled? Would you feel accomplished even without putting in daily groundwork of achieving your goals? What you put into your life, you can expect to receive. The law of compensation rewards those who are willing to put forth the effort. In order to achieve greatness, you need to build a foundation first. The foundation should be built around your purpose, and will always take precedence over the end goal. When you have the right vision, the universe will line itself up, and the end goal becomes inevitable. Wealth would be the effect of becoming fulfilled. You can have all the money in the world, but you will never become fulfilled unless you establish a foundation first. It all begins with a single step.

The journey is the greatest gift you will ever experience. During this process, you will attract people into your life who are searching for similar meaning. These connections will impact the developmental stage of your journey. New experiences will equate to new ways of finding joy and happiness, enabling you to keep focused on the path you set forth for yourself. Any obstacles or personal setbacks are part of the process. These minor defeats enable you to shift gears and refocus your plan. With the shift in awareness, you will gain clarity on your vision. As long as you pursue your passion with proper intention, you will realize you would not have been able to reach your desires without the hurdles along the way.

The universe is sending constant reminders, as if it is whispering in your ear, redirecting you back onto your path towards your purpose. It is always working in your favor, even when you stumble. As you become aware of these signs, you will realize how to respond. Oftentimes, we struggle with perseverance. We have been taught to persevere through adversity until we reach our goal. However, sometimes the universe has a better plan for you. If you continue forcing something when it does not feel natural, you will be chasing your tail, trying to reach for something that is not in the cards for you. For example, if your goal is to become an Olympic swimmer and break all the records set by Michael Phelps, but you've never swum a competitive race in your life, you have to ask yourself if this feels natural. The perseverance and hard work will enable you to become a great swimmer, but your ego is blocking you from refocusing your energy on something that IS natural to you. As you become more aware, you will determine your ego has been controlling your decisions. Your ego is your resistance. The habits you set forth for yourself will continue to follow you around until you listen to the universe, break your ego, and pivot from your current plan of action. Resistance will lead to further displeasure.

Bad experiences will lead to positive outcomes when you recognize how the universe is working in your favor. Minor setbacks, which may appear major at the time, are necessary in order to gain a broader perspective. Every time you switch careers/jobs, there is something to be gained by the experience, and you will find that you are on a stepping-stone to a greater purpose. The universe is redirecting you through your subconscious mind, which is greater than your current imagination. Your desires may seem unimaginable today, but as you shift your awareness to a higher frequency, your imagination evolves within it, eliminating limitations you had placed in your subconscious mind. Your imagination becomes greater with more experiences, which inform your shift to higher consciousness.

As you continue unlocking doors from your subconscious mind, you will gradually have these awakening experiences without fully realizing it at the time. They appear to be little epiphanies, one after another. These moments become gateways towards your higher self. As you continue to climb your way through this journey, you will be rewarded with events that bring you joy, fulfillment, and happiness.

When you are able to express yourself, your spirit will embody free will. Challenge yourself in areas where you lack competence. The limitations you created for yourself years ago do not exist today. Engage with activities that are stimulating and leave you inspired. The amount of fulfilment you receive will never quantify to a dollar amount.

Upon returning home from a lengthy holiday break, shortly after having my first real awakening experience, I could not get comfortable in my own home. I had already been living there for about eight years, but it was the first time I could not get comfortable. I was turned off by the interior design, and the ambiance did not match my frequency. I had never experienced a renovation project due to fear, but I decided to kick my apprehension aside and begin my first renovation. Throwing paint on the wall, ripping up old carpet, adding hardwood floors, and buying décor for the place was the first free-spirited and uplifting experience I had ever had. I was in love with the freedom and the ability to express myself, breaking free from the prison I found myself in, thinking I was not capable of such a task. I was having an out-of-body experience, one with passion I had never felt before.

Upon reflection, this experience would have not happened if I did not experience significant setbacks of my own. My inexperience in the stock market was the catalyst behind this awakening. Thinking I could make a living trading on the stock market after less than a year of proper training led to a financial setback. If I had started out trading successfully in the stock market, I likely would not have renovated the house myself, and probably would have hired someone to do the job for me. This enlightening experience led to the explosion of my imagination, which inevitably led to the expansion of my mind.

Jumping Off a Sinking Ship Is Part of the Process

After early success with short-term rentals, I took on a business venture in short-term property rentals with a friend from college (which will be discussed in greater detail in chapter 14). As much as I wanted the business plan to work, the universe had a better plan. I had imagined this partnership being something that we would grow together from, feeding off of each other's momentum. I suggested we start with one property, and preserve the earnings so we could add new properties to our portfolio. Over time, the partnership began to weaken. Every time we seemed to be getting out of the "red" and making money, we would experience another setback.

Reflecting back on it now, breaking free from the partnership was the best thing that could have happened. It was an experience my ego failed to acknowledge during the time; however, the universe kept sending me regular messages throughout the journey as to why I should not be in this partnership. Since it is impossible to multi-task, I found myself paying more attention to a sinking ship than working towards my personal goals and vision. As I kept thinking of new ways to generate revenue for our newly formed partnership, the universe continued sending reminders that this was not the ideal situation to grow. After selling the property and ending the part-nership once and for all, I began to see immediate growth in my personal and professional life. I was no longer consumed by the part-nership, but instead, I began focusing on my own ventures.

After being fortunate to break free from the experience, rela-tively unscathed, I was able to utilize my time and expand on an-other short-term property rental business with a new partner at a fraction of the cost. Also, with the abundance of free time on my hands, I found myself researching new ways to grow my business, reading a lot more, working on my mental and spiritual well-being, and discovering the path of my journey. The universe was speak-ing to me through the experiences of the stock market debacle and failed partnership, placing me on the right path towards my purpose, something that would have not been achieved had I "persevered" through adversity. Both of these ventures became great learning ex-periences, and made me look deep inside and question everything around me. The moment that I gave myself time and listened to the universe, I started hearing answers. As these examples were drawn out over time, without understanding "why" in the moment, I knew there was always a reason for everything. If you resist the messag-es being sent to you, you are inadvertently strengthening your ego while weakening your awareness.

Listening Versus Ignoring the Universe

Observe the signals the universe is sending you. What are the mes-sages that are being sent? How are you receiving these messages? When you respond appropriately to these signals, it will draw you closer to achieving your desires. If you ignore these messages, you will not evolve from your current situation. We live in a friendly universe, so our universe is working for you, not against you.

Observe how these messages can work for you. Imagine that you have been working in the field of dentistry since you were 16 years old as a dental assistant. After moving across the country, you find a great position at a nearby dentist office. Your desire is to eventually become a dental hygienist at this office, but the turnover rate is extremely low; there has not been a new dental hygienist hired in this office in over five years. Since you are fascinated by everything about the field, you decide to leave your current position and pursue your dream of becoming a dental hygienist.

After a long, strenuous program, you are coming close to graduation. As this happens, you hear a rumor that a hygienist at the office where you used to work is about to move out of state and the position will need to be filled. Upon graduation, the office you used to work for is ready to hire you. This does not happen by luck. There are no coincidences.

You are creating your own luck by visualizing your desires, which then manifests into reality. By having a plan, and putting your plan into action, you will ultimately reach your end goal. Once the end goal is reached, you will discover the journey was the best part of the process. Not only did you graduate with a dental hygiene degree, your parents surprised you and attended your graduation ceremony, and watched you win the Golden Scaler Award as the most outstanding student in the graduating class. Anything is possible. You just have to know what you want, visualize it being in your possession, put the plan into action, follow the messages from the universe, and respond appropriately.

When you fail to listen to the universe, you will be stuck in the same position you are currently in for the rest of your life. For example, if you aspire to become an interior designer, and have a special talent but are afraid of losing out on the benefits from a high-paying job, then follow the messages the universe is sending. If your goal is to start your own interior design business, and share your talents with the rest of the world by using social media as a platform, visualize what you want and the right person may come along.

While attending a private party, you come across someone who has been an interior designer for 30+ years and is looking to retire.

You have two choices: engage or don't engage. This is the universe putting you in a position to fulfill your desires. The universe put you there for a reason. Begin the process by taking the interior designer out for coffee or lunch. Interview them about their profession, and ask what they love about it and why they chose it as a career. Build on this conversation and see where it leads. Discover what you can do for yourself today without sacrificing your permanent job in order to get started. If you do not initiate further guidance, you may never know when the universe will put you on this direct path again.

Every new inquiry is a stepping stone to get you where you need to be. As you continue to ignore the messages the universe is sending, you will eventually become desensitized to your YOU. You will never become fulfilled, and will live life with resentment. You will have a sense of displacement and nothing will ever feel right. Nothing ever falls into your lap. Just because you visualize what you want does not mean it will happen for you. The law of attraction will put these messages directly in your path, but the "action" through the law of vibration will guide you towards your destiny. Do not expect it to be wrapped in a box with a pretty bow with a tag that says "Your future resides in this box. Open me at once." Because it will not happen. Open up your intuitive nature and acknowledge the events that fall into your path, and be willing to accept them as they happen.

You have a vision of how you are going to obtain your goals. Walk your path alone, and do not worry what other people say. Sometimes you have to start over in life and make a lot of changes, whether it be moving to another city or state, changing relationships, or a new job. Understand that in order to manifest your desires, you will have to make sacrifices along the way. You may have to move in with a family member and sleep on the couch. You may need to turn down high-paying jobs because they do not serve your purpose. Your YOU and the universe are collaborating on a plan together. Follow the flow of the universe and you will prevail.

CHAPTER FIVE

THE POWER BEHIND YOUR IMAGINATION

Law of Attraction

You have the power to create anything you want in life. If it can be imagined, it can be achieved. Remember when you were a young child and had a magical imagination? Anything was possible. Kids believe in miracles such as Santa Claus, the Easter Bunny, and the Tooth Fairy. Faith was real. Possibilities were endless. Then you were taught what you can and cannot do, or what is real and what is "fake." We begin to question whether or not faith is real or if we simply need to live with the hand that we were dealt. Slowly but surely, what was a burning flame of desire, our imagination, dwindles down to candlelight flame around the dinner table before eventually burning out. We are told what to believe and what to expect as we live in a system of rules, and if we accept that, then that is what we manifest.

We live in a society made up of rules and structure, created by people that are not any smarter than us. The only difference is they believed it would work, and sure enough, it did. Humans are not meant to be confined by a set of rules that interfere with our nature. These restrictions put us in a bubble and we begin to make excuses as to why we will never achieve certain things in life. We live with this mindset because we have been told our entire life by others what to think, so we accept it as our way of life. As we continue to live this pattern, we are attracting this lifestyle by the way we think. Instead of finding reasons why you can't, start to find reasons why you can. You will begin to manifest anything and everything you ever wanted in your life because of one law: The Law of Attraction.

Everything you have ever experienced in your life was received because of the law of attraction. Rhonda Byrne, author of the best-selling book, *The Secret*, said,

> "The law of attraction is a law of nature. It is impersonal and it does not see good things or bad things. It is receiving your thoughts and reflecting back to you those thoughts as your life experience. The law of attraction simply gives you whatever it is you are thinking about."

The law of attraction simply gives you whatever it is you are thinking about.

Have you ever thought of something only to see it come true in a matter of minutes, days, weeks, months, or years? What you focus on, good or bad, is being attracted to you based on the signals you are sending out in the universe. These signals send a frequency, similar to the frequency of a radio. The frequency places you on the path to whatever it is you are thinking at the time. Through repetitive thought, you continue to raise your frequency, placing you on a direct path for what you are attracting. Without proper action, you will prevent yourself from attracting certain things into your life. The proper action can only occur through your vibration.

Law of Vibration

You will not be able to achieve a goal simply by visualizing a new idea and expecting it to manifest into your reality. Visualizing what you are determined to accomplish raises your frequency, but it will not manifest without proper action. The last 6 letters of "attraction" are "action." You cannot attract what you want without proper action. In order to manifest your desires, you need to follow the most important law: law of vibration. We live in an "ocean of motion" and are sending messages out into the universe, which create your frequency. The action you take is your vibration. A pond at rest remains at rest until you cast a stone, creating a ripple effect. The same act of vibration works for you. The law of vibration, simply put, is putting your plan into action. Once you begin putting your plan into action, you are transforming your energy towards intention, casting a ripple effect throughout the universe. You must continue to follow through with your plan of action to allow the flow of vibration to take place. Each time you raise your vibration, you become a magnet for attracting new opportunities, opportunities that were not available prior to the initial action taking place. The universe will show you the way, but it is up to you to take action.

Sometimes it may feel as though you are pushing a boulder up the side of a mountain, like you are barely making any progress. Since you are only inching slightly higher each time, you become discouraged at the lack of immediate results. However, when you look back from where you started, you will see how far along you have come in a relatively short period of time. Once you have created a habit for yourself, you have reconditioned your subconscious mind to raise your awareness, inevitably raising your frequency and vibration in the process.

Like the action of the stock market: you will have some good days and some bad days. However, whenever you have a bad day, remember where you were before you first started. Your current lows may have been your old highs. Therefore, when you are feeling down, do not let it discourage you from achieving greatness. Consider it a consolidation period like the stock market, and regather your position, using your old highs as your new floor and a place to pivot. You have already come a long way from where you started; therefore, do not let one minor setback prevent you from reaching your goals.

You are the creator of your universe. What you thought could not be possible when you first started suddenly became impossible to give up. Michael Jordan and Kobe Bryant did not become the greatest basketball players of all time simply by visualizing what they wanted. They put in the work. They went to the gym and practiced when others were going to clubs or sleeping. Nothing happens by accident. When you apply intention and determination towards your focus, your manifestation unfolds before you as if it is pulling you by the wrist towards your purpose. The amount of thought, visualization, and action you apply into manifesting your desires, the law of compensation will reward you equally in return. There is no such thing as "luck." Luck = preparedness + opportunity. Create your own luck, and you will see greatness manifest right before your eyes.

Believe it CAN Happen

Mork and Mindy was my favorite show when I was a child. I believed life existed on other planets and galaxies, which were more evolved than our world. This show helped me discover the true meaning of imagination and what you can achieve. One of my favorite segments of the show was when Mork took an egg out of the egg carton and performed a trick to have the egg fly away. I was convinced I could do the same thing under the right circumstances. When I rushed over to the refrigerator, I pulled out the eggs and began my experiment. By the time the second egg landed on the ground, my mother rushed over, took the eggs, and ruined my experiment. This did not sit well with me, so I knew I needed to create a diversion.

A little later, I thought of the perfect storm. Somehow my twin brother, Billy, and I arranged a plan to pour maple syrup over his head. When my mom rushed my brother into the bathroom to clean him off, I found the perfect opportunity to continue with my experiment. I proceeded to make my way back to the kitchen and opened the refrigerator door. While the shower was still running, I knew I had all the time in the world to complete my experiment. By the fourth attempt, with the fifth egg in my hand, my mom had this maternal intuitive instinct that something was too quiet with me. She rushed back into the kitchen to discover my experiment. It was a success! I learned that it is impossible to have eggs from my refrigerator fly! My experiments did not end there.

I grew up believing I had the most significant imagination possible. Whatever I thought of, I felt that it could happen. Another time, when I was in second grade watching a puppet show in the gymnasium, I was sitting in the front row watching Jack and the Beanstalk. The puppeteers threw "magic beans" through their set and scattered amongst the children in the audience. I was so excited that I caught one! Without telling anyone for fear of being told "no," I took it home and planted it in my backyard. I imagined growing the biggest beanstalk ever and expected to ask for forgiveness once it took shape. The experiment was also a success! The beanstalk did not grow, but my imagination did not dwindle from there. I was determined to explore all possibilities to decide for myself what would work and what would not. I felt as though if I believed in something, it could be achieved.

I never felt any of my failed experiments were a failure. I saw it as a learned experience. Thomas Edison did not fail 10,000 times when inventing the incandescent lightbulb. He *learned* 10,000 ways not to invent a lightbulb. Every creation starts with imagination. Steve Jobs, who was the inventor of Apple, imagined a device that could hold 10,000 songs. In 2001, he created the iPod, a digital device to hold music in the palm of your hand. He later expanded his vision with the iPhone that is widely used today.

What we use in today's world seems normal but would have seemed like alien technology 100 years ago. No one believed you could take something that weighs 487.5 tons and make it fly until the Wright brothers invented the first airplane in 1903. Technology has become so advanced today that it seems unimaginable in today's generation to not have it. I did not have the internet until I graduated high school in 1997, and now I cannot imagine life without it. Everything that exists today may have seemed unimaginable to the majority of the population 100 years ago. Imagine what can be achieved once you use your imagination. Everything can come to fruition, and all you have to do is take the first step, and that is to believe.

There Are No Limits on What YOU Can Do

Our imagination and creativity can become limited while we are being programmed. From the time we are born, we are continually told what our limitations are and are expected to conform to the norms in society. We have minimal control from when we are born to age 7 over how we behave. This is the timeframe our subconscious is being developed. We become a reflection of our environment and learn by imitating others, especially our parents, siblings, family members, and people we see at church and school. While our brain is being hardwired, our limitations become self-imposed. We become a reflection of the world around us starting at a very young age.

Knowledge is powerful, but it can have its limitations. Henry Ford, the first to produce affordable cars for the general public, which revolutionized the transportation industry, did not exceed an 8th-grade education. George Washington, the first president of the United States, did not achieve higher than a 5th-grade education. Bill Gates, founder of Microsoft, and Mark Zuckerberg, founder of Facebook, did not graduate from college. Marshall Mathers, better known as Eminem, winner of 15 Grammy Awards, was the first hip-hop artist to win an Academy Award, never graduated high school. These are only a few examples of people who felt their schooling provided them with limitations rather than a path to abundance. Their imagination led to their success, not the amount of education they had.

Not to dismiss what having a proper education can do for you, but your imagination becomes limited when you think the only thing you need in life is proper education. Education does not equate experience. The knowledge that you receive today is a building block to unlocking your true potential, but your imagination is the only thing that can make it possible. If you can imagine it, it can be achieved.

Look at all the visionaries of the past and present: Thomas Edison, Nikola Tesla, Henry Ford, Denzel Washington, Oprah Winfrey, and Elon Musk are all great examples that chose not to be limited by what they were told to believe. They took their imagination to a higher level and achieved something that would seem impossible to others because of what they envisioned.

I was enjoying the journey of life while in grade school. When I graduated high school, I had no clue what I wanted to do. While I was in college, I still did not find the answers I was looking for and began to feel pressure on what I should be doing with my life. When I thought that I had to choose what I wanted to become, I felt this attraction as if I was being pulled in the direction of the entertainment industry. I loved performing and being on stage, whether it was in a play or karaoke night at a local pub.

I completed the required courses to earn a major in communications with a minor in theater and film. All I ever imagined I would be doing after college was performing on stage or in movies or TV shows.

Just prior to graduation, I was drawn to Eminem's style and performance. Eminem was the most significant act in hip-hop at the time, and I found myself going to karaoke bars and emulating his voice, stage presence, and style. I would learn his music, find the hardest song on his newest albums, and practice until I could do it, or at least come close to it. I imagined how amazing it would be if I could collaborate with this legendary artist one way or the other.

Believe in Fate

As a young kid full of hope, my imagination was unlimited. I was never comfortable being told what my limitations were. I felt whatever I wanted to do, I could achieve. I rarely closed the door on an experience which led me to becoming a cheerleader during my freshman year of college. During the 2001 season, heading into the 5th year with the team, we got a new coach. The new coach switched my stunt partner to another person, and I was assigned to someone who had never stunted before. My ego got in the way and I was not interested in spending my 5th year relearning the basics, so I was bitter about the move.

During the off-season, our team was working a bunch of fundraiser events, including working concessions at Detroit Tigers games and opera performances at Tiger Stadium. A new fundraising event took place at the Michigan International Speedway in Belle Isle, a venue I had never been to.

I printed out the directions from MapQuest and was on my way to the event. While I was driving there, I was blinded by the sunrise, causing me to miss my turn. As I entered a neighborhood, I realized that I had missed my exit somewhere along the way. When I turned around to head back, the sun was behind me, and I was able to see the turn I should have made 20 minutes earlier. I did not really think much about being late for the event. I figured I could just jump on board and work with my team when I arrived. It was common for team members to be a little late to one of these functions, since we had to be there hours in advance.

When I arrived, I saw many of my teammates stationed in different sections of the tents. Our new coach did not attend this function due to a previous engagement, so I was looking for the person in charge. When I found this person, who I had never met before, he began yelling at me. Immediately, his vibe rubbed me the wrong way. He said to me in a condescending tone, "Because you were late, you will be replenishing every station with food and drinks when they run low throughout the event."

He was unaware of a nagging back injury I was dealing with, so I informed him I would not be able to perform these tasks. He immediately fired back at me, saying, "You're just mad you're not going to be working with your friends! You're going to stay here and work!" I was like, oh hell no. I did not even respond to his accusations. Instead, I took off my apron, extended my arm to hand it back to him. He did not reach for the apron. He said, "You're staying, and you're going to work!" Without hesitation, I dropped the apron at his feet, and began walking away. He continued to yell at me, saying, "You're not going anywhere!"

Completely ignoring his commands, I kept walking. I knew that walking away would not look good for the team, nor reflect well on myself. I figured I would receive a reprimand from the coach once she heard my side of the story. Walking away was the freest I had ever felt. I had felt controlled by an employer, team, organization, school, etc., and for the first time in a long while, I felt like I had control of life and the choices I made. I was content to let fate decide my future when it came to my 5th year of the cheerleading team.

I arrived at practice on the following Tuesday, where I was greeted by the new coach. Instead of pulling me aside, she chewed me out in front of the team, and sided with the supervisor at the event. When I tried to explain my side of the story, she said that the supervisor said I was "late" and referred to me as a "bad apple" and said I should be disciplined. I found it hysterical and attempted to explain what had happened.

Without hearing my side of the story, she said, "You're suspended indefinitely." I said, "Ok, what does that mean?" She said, "When you show genuine remorse for your actions, I will allow you to rejoin the team." I did not know how I could show remorse when I felt like the supervisor was condemning me for being late. Other teammates had been suspended for a couple weeks before, but apparently, this suspension was unprecedented. I no longer had any desire to see it through. When I left practice, it was the second time I felt free. I did not know what to do with my extra time. I was feeling burnt out from the team, and was looking forward to seeing where my free time would take me.

I started the indefinite suspension at the beginning of the fall, during football season. I enjoyed the abundance of free time. Practices were every Tuesday, Thursday, and Sunday, with football games on Saturday.

A few of my theater friends asked me if I planned on going to the open casting call for "Eminem's movie." At the time, it was referred to as the "Untitled Detroit Project," later known as *8 Mile*. After learning that I could either attend the casting call on Saturday or Sunday, I was amazed by the coincidence of the timing. If I had still been on the cheerleading team, I wouldn't have been able to attend either of the casting calls.

I decided to attend the casting call on Sunday with a couple of my theater friends. When I arrived, we were required to fill out a little questionnaire on a 5X7 blue card, stating our credentials. As I was filling out the card, I highlighted my film and theater minor as a part of my experience. Otherwise, my experience was basically non-existent.

I imagined how cool it would be to be an "extra" and gain a glimpse of Eminem, who had achieved so much fame in a short period of time. I was interested to see the aura that came with his fame. I thought it would be a longshot if I earned a role in the movie, but was expecting to be called for an extras role in one of the scenes. I envisioned myself getting the opportunity to meet the Grammy Award–winning actor, and felt the excitement as if it had already happened.

On Wednesday, later that week, I came home from school midday to take my customary nap. My roommate, Buddy, yelled for me while I was upstairs in my room and said, "Tony! I know how much you hate to be awakened from your naps, but Universal Studios is on the phone!" My eyes opened wider than they had ever opened before. I thought to myself, wow, they are very efficient. They had said they wouldn't need extras for a couple months, so maybe they were gauging interest for specific days.

I took the call from the extras casting director. She said, "It looks like you have experience in film and acting, and we would like you to audition to be Marshall Mathers's (Eminem's) stand-in. Are you available?"

I said, "Yes! So, you need me to be an extra in the film?"

She said, "No. You will be a stand-in for Marshall Mathers for the entire filming process, so you will need to be available every day he is on the set. Are you available?"

It was October, and I was in the middle of taking 18 credits that semester. I had my eyes set on graduating the following semester. Without hesitation, I said, "Yes!"

She replied, "We need to see if you will work out well with the cast and crew. Since we spend a lot of time together, they become 'like family,' and we need to make sure you are a good fit. Does this sound like you?"

I said, "Of course it does! I'm excited to start. When do you need me?"

Once I got the time and place, I went to Google to learn what a stand-in is and what it does. I learned that a stand-in takes the actor's place on set, blocking out the scene with the other stand-ins and extras while the crew sets up the background, lighting, and camera angles. During the setup, the director of photography and casting director look through the viewfinder to see how the shot will look once the talent returns to the set. It was astounding to me that I was literally going to be Eminem's stand-in and work side-by-side with the legend himself, manifesting quicker than imagined.

I arrived on the set and learned that Eminem would not be there that day. The objective for the first day of filming was to test the filters, lighting, and background lighting to see how it would look through the camera, using myself and Mekhi Phifer's stand-in. It was an audition for me, so I made sure I had a decent set of clothes on, and a pair of Timberlands to make myself an inch taller after learning Eminem was an inch taller than me.

The first day of filming went very well. They asked me to come back the following day and asked if I wouldn't mind cutting my hair. I had no problem with the request at all. I was excited about how well everything had gone and could not wait to come back the following day. Everyone was great and easy to get along with, especially the director of photography, or cinematographer, Rodrigo Prieto, who realized that I had minimal acting experience in a motion picture, and coached me along the way, helping me understand what to expect. I was grateful for his support, without which I would not have made it past the first week of filming.

The following day of filming was going to be the most significant opportunity at this stage in my life. I was about to meet Eminem, which would allow the Academy Award–winning director, Curtis Hanson, to determine if I was a good fit. Eminem was battling a brief illness that day, so he was expected to arrive on set a little bit late. Meeting the actors seemed surreal to me and I was glad to break the seal with Brittany Murphy. She was the sweetest and kindest person I'd ever met. While we were sitting in the holding room together, I expressed my nervousness about meeting Eminem. She said to just be natural and not to worry. I said I worried how I may come off to him and did not want to jeopardize this opportunity. She reassured me that she met a ton of celebrities, and that Eminem was cool, and would be happy to meet me.

She was right! While Brittany Murphy's stand-in and I were standing in front of the camera during the screen tests, she whispered to me, "There's Eminem." Thankfully we were 10 feet away, and I was able to maintain my balance and composure. It felt like a dream, similar to what I had imagined.

Moments later, Eminem was brought around to the other side of the camera, where I was formally introduced. I bottled up and maintained my composure, extended my arm, and mumbled, "Nice to meet you, Marshall." Seconds later, we were asked to stand back-to-back to see if I was a perfect match. Knowing he was an inch taller, wearing taller shoes, I took a deep breath to gain a little extra height. I heard Rodrigo say, "Looks like we got a good match." Curtis said, "Yeah, I agree." I was relieved, but still nervous as we began filming.

All the excitement I had experienced, along with being overjoyed with emotion, was still bottled up inside of me. I did not want to come off as a crazed, obsessed fan because I was in the moment of living out two dreams: meeting a legend, and working on a major motion picture with an Academy Award–winning director. Everything seemed surreal, but had manifested greater than I had originally imagined.

After making it through the first day of meeting Eminem, we had a day off, on Eminem's birthday, before beginning the actual filming of the movie the very next day. When we started filming on October 18, 2001, it was a shortened day. We shot the scene, "Hey Sol... when you gotta stop living up here, and start living down here." This message was extremely significant to me at this point in my life. I felt like I had achieved "living up here" by being in the position I was in.

The day before we began filming, I overheard Eminem say to Curtis that he was nervous about filming. Curtis replied, "Why?" I didn't hear much after that, but it helped me feel comfortable that someone in his position was equally nervous as someone like me. We were in the same boat at different levels in our life. To make matters more nerve-racking for me, the behind-the-scenes camera was on set the first day of filming, directly pointed at me. I was in an undersized jacket to match Eminem's wardrobe in a car scene, and Eminem was to my right, with Curtis and Rodrigo to my left. I had no idea what was going on and almost panicked. I looked over to my left at Curtis and Rodrigo to seem more engaged with them, as if I knew what was going on, rather than reacting to Eminem standing to my right. I played it off perfectly.

Allow Your Imagination to Manifest Your Desires

Imagination is one of our most significant powers. It can be used to create something from nothing, change a negative situation into a positive one, and redirect your overall mood. It is essential to be consistent with how you use the power of your imagination. When you use the potential for positive purposes, you will place yourself on a path for positive events. When you use your imaginative power to create negative thoughts, particularly in hypothetical scenarios, like "the world is coming to an end," and visualize the worst, the worst is likely to happen because the universe is mirroring your thoughts.

While I was working on the set, I wanted to be one of the actors rather than hiding behind the scenes. Instead of appreciating my current position and taking everything in, I began to want more. When my desire turned into wanting more, I was telling the universe what I did not have. I had a conversation with Brittany Murphy that changed my attitude.

It was common to strike up a conversation with the actors on the set. When I was sharing my desire with Brittany about being in front of the camera, rather than being behind the scenes, I was worried that my position could be easily replaced. The insecurities I had about having something significant taken from me due to inexperience alarmed me. I figured if I had a leading role on a film, that it would be more difficult to find a replacement, especially once the film had already been shot.

After sharing my thoughts with her, she said, "We cannot film this movie without you." I said, "I'm easily replaceable. You're not." She said something that really hit home with me and changed the way I viewed any position in life. She said, "I'm just as replaceable as you, and we could not film this without any one of us."

I was taken aback by her comments. For the first time, I understood my value and what I meant, not only to my family, but to people I connect with. The value you provide to your environment has a significant impact on the choices you make.

Everything that transpired, from the events leading up to the casting call to years after the movie was released, had manifested because of my imagination. The power of your imagination can bring you the greatest gifts in life. All you have to do is visualize it, feel it, follow the messages from the universe, stay on the path, then receive it. Feel it as if it is already in your possession, and you will receive it. When the events leading up to it come into fruition, the feeling you already have from accepting the gift will be as if you already possessed it, and you will know how to respond.

Stay the Course

On several occasions, my imagination manifested into my desires. Whatever the step of the process was, I felt compelled to focus attention on what brought me joy, striving into deeper fulfillment. However, I was met with many obstacles along the way without always seeing the big picture due to sheer ignorance.

Early on, like many, I was commonly distracted by urges that did not serve a purpose, oftentimes shifting my focus away from what was important. Even though in the heat of the moment it felt like a need, I ultimately realized that they were distractions. Whether it was a job that did not provide advancing opportunities, an incompatible relationship, an education I did not value, or weekend celebrations beginning on Thursday night and ending on "Sunday-Fun-Day," I steered away from my purpose, losing my identity in the process. It felt like "everyone's doing it" so I had to conform to what was expected of me.

It is important to see these distractions quickly and shift gears to focus your energy on something that brings value, something I was beginning to understand when using the power of imagination, even in my youth. I still was not quite sure how the law of attraction worked, but I was quite optimistic in every situation, and it seemed like I received everything I wanted in life simply by visualizing it.

It is impossible to have a dream come into existence without applying proper action. The law of vibration states that we attract our thoughts and can achieve through appropriate action. As Paulo Coelho from *The Alchemist* said, "When you want something, all the universe conspires in helping you achieve it." The synchronicity of events had to unfold before me to land the role as Eminem's stand-in. Choosing to be positive after being met with misfortune led to being in the right place at the right time and landing the part.

Unfortunately, far too often, people defer to negative behaviors when facing adversity. Oftentimes, people use their hardship as an excuse for their current position. Pessimism will almost always lead to misery and misfortune, because it is the current vibration that is being sent out to the universe.

Be careful what you speak out into the universe. It is always listening. Whether you imagine something positive or negative, either will unfold before you. The frequency you lay before you will align your path with what you wish to achieve. Your imagination develops deep in your subconscious like a seed planted in a garden, waiting to be nourished. It will manifest through repetitive thought and action. Without proper development, it will stay what it is – a dream.

The power of imagination is so powerful that you could find yourself caught in someone else's imagination and it could become your reality. You have control over yourself, but when you become entangled in the process, particularly during the developmental stage, the forces of imagination with people in your environment become so strong that it can influence your journey. By placing yourself in the right environment, with the right friends, co-workers, clients, your path to your imagination is controlled by your situations and who you choose to associate with.

You have been attracting these people since the day you were born. Your pattern of behavior has been a compilation of events on top of events that have snowballed to where you are today. How you engage within your environment spirals into a life of its own. Oftentimes you have control of your environment, but usually, you do not have the same control at a younger age since you cannot choose your family, but you can control your inner circle.

I found myself caught in the web of my dad's imagination, entangled by his desires. He had planted the seed in Billy's and my subconscious as early as we can remember that we must graduate college, and continued to imagine it until it became a reality. Billy and I both graduated because we manifested his thoughts into his reality which became our reality. His imaginings were often stubborn, but he always had good intentions for what he wanted.

My mother imagined being a mom and was determined to be the best there ever was. When it came to nurturing, listening, support, companionship, and love, my mom's will for her kids could be felt from all over. All of us knew she would be there for us, no matter what. When we got into trouble, she supported us, helping us learn from our mistakes. She never showed any disappointment for anything we ever did. She was always proud of us or saw each mistake as part of life, a new opportunity to grow and develop from. Her imagination evolved into becoming the heart of the house, a nurturing and warm environment that we were lucky to have.

Just because you have an imagination about something, does not mean it will pan out exactly how you anticipated. You are going to have a lot of bumps along the way, and have new experiences you did not think possible. This is all part of the learning process. Sometimes, you have to get knocked down to build a foundation to prepare for where your imagination leads you. Once you have a solid foundation in place, you will begin the next phase of your journey.

Once you accomplish your desire, you may discover the journey was more rewarding than the destination. Reflect on the journey and the obstacles you overcame. What do you feel you gained after experiencing temporary defeat? Repeat the process and decide where you want your path to take you next. Feel the vision as if you own it. Let it come to you in your life. Take the path that feels right and least resistant, and focus on your next destination. By taking this path, you will achieve anything that you set your mind to.

If you imagine your path being difficult, you can bet your path will be a challenge. When you expect to reach the path of your desired destination, sit back and look around, and watch the events from the universe unfold before you. The inevitable is your destination. The path that you take starts with your imagination. How you respond to adversity and benchmarks determines the outcome. The more positive you are, the more you will enjoy the journey. Life is a marathon, not a sprint. When you are doing something that you love every day of your life, you will not feel the need to retire. Make every day feel like a Saturday, and you will never work a day in your life.

Even though you have a path for yourself, others may also have a path for you. You may find yourself gravitating to their frequency if it is more comfortable or the path of least resistance. To break off the path of someone else's frequency, create the path for yourself, and discover what you need to do to get through the easiest path as often as possible.

A parent may want you to become a lawyer. A teacher may think you would make a great accountant. A friend may push you into becoming a coach. A teammate might think you will make the NFL. You should always steer clear if you do not have the desire for what someone else wants you to be. If you do not find passion in the suggested field, you will not enjoy pursuing it as a career.

You can attract anything you want in life. Your imagination

is the key ingredient to achieving your goal. If you have negative thoughts and think of the worst-case scenario, you will find yourself in the path of unfortunate events. The cycle will continue until you change the way you think.

When you have positive thoughts, regardless of what life throws your way, you can be assured that what is happening will put you on the path to your desires. Every sidestep, detour, or misdirection happens to put you in line with your frequency and vibration, inevitably directing you towards your goals, so imagine big.

When you imagine having something in your life, does it come true because you expected to receive it? Was it a new bike? The job you always wanted? An 'A' on a math test? Chances are you did. Prior to accomplishing your goal, you had already visualized what it would be like once you received it and had the feeling of it already in your possession. Once you acquire the feeling of acceptance through visualization, it becomes as good as yours.

Upon receiving your goal, reflect on what you did to receive it. What events led up to achieving your goal? What detours did you take? How did you respond while the events were happening? Were you positive or negative? What was your imagination like? Did you feel like you already possessed it without actually possessing it?

When you feel as though you are already in possession of something, you will realize your imagination is the key ingredient. All you have to do is put your thoughts into action through the law of vibration. When you dream of winning the lottery, you cannot expect to win without purchasing a lottery ticket. If you imagine yourself being an actor or singer, you will not be in any performances without proper training, experience, and attending auditions. What you desire in life begins from your imagination, all beginning with a single step.

The universe is constantly sending you messages in response to your actions. What you put out in the universe comes back to you, whether it is positive or negative. If you feel you have been positive, and something bad happens, this is the universe redirecting you in favor of your path, not against you. The universe can be sending you signals, whether it be in your sleep, at the grocery store, meeting someone at the gym, a random thought that enters your mind, or through adversity. It always finds a way to send symbolic messages to become the person you are destined to be.

The people that you have in your life, the events that occur, the temptations to resist, are all reflections to guide you towards your path. When you keep making the right choice and follow the flow of positive energy around you, ignoring and blocking the negative energy from entering your life, you will achieve your true purpose. When you are passionate and love who you become, you will express gratitude for what you have, attracting more abundance in your life while having a clear sense of identity.

Do not let things enter your life that are out of your control affect your mood. When you allow it to affect your mood, it will change your attitude and how you view things. Once the pattern is set, it becomes tough to break. Always forgive. A person who has a negative mindset developed their habits over a long period of time, and forgot how to be positive. You only have control over yourself. Lead by example and do not engage in someone's negative way of thinking.

Create an environment that helps you to flourish. Whether it is at work, home, a coffee shop, a library, outside walking in nature or on the beach, put yourself in an environment to eliminate distractions from those trying to throw you off your path. Others around you can feel your energy, and when your frequency is raised, people around you subconsciously see and feel the aura you cast. If they are not adding to your frequency, then be aware that they might be trying to take your energy. Do not let these people into your life and always focus on yourself.

When you love yourself first, your love will emanate into those around you. Your passion for what you are doing, the things you own, your environment and surroundings are the most powerful force you can give out into the universe. When you keep sending out love, you will continue receiving love because it becomes a part of you.

Throughout your journey, you will experience things coming and going in your life, with many things appearing fake. These are illusions, attempting to misdirect you like when a magician performs a magic trick. A person's ego is an illusion. The ego is a self-created avatar of someone, created by themselves, and amplified by those around them when they feed into it. Illusions are found in politics, media coverage, social media, the education system, and all other methods that are used to control the general population.

When you are becoming the person you are destined to be, be aware of things that happen in your life that might feel unnatural. When it feels like you're being pulled by the wrist and directed where to go, and you feel resistance, trust your instincts. Your intuition and subconscious are more powerful than you realize, and are working for you.

Not all people are the same. Every person is unique in their own particular way. Being crafted in a cookie-cutter system goes against your true nature. The discovery in finding your true purpose is a tremendous path, and a fun journey as long as you are willing to allow it. Follow the signs the universe is sending, keep your imagination infinite, and let the pieces unfold before you. Your imagination is so powerful that if you can visualize it, it can be achieved. You have to feel your imagination as if it is already in your possession. The only limits that exist are the ones in your own mind. Use your mind to achieve anything you want. In the process, you will FIND YOUR YOU!

Chapter Six

THE EGO

I miss my mom calling me "Mitch." It was short for "midget" because I was very little when I was young. It never felt harsh when she called me it. In fact, I loved it. It made me feel special and unique. Everyone has a name. My mom gave me something special, something exclusive, something that was...ME!

One day, my mom and I were out shopping, and she referred to me as "Mitch." I was in a cranky mood and said, "Don't call me that anymore!" It made her feel bad. A month or so went by and I asked why she'd stopped calling me "Mitch." She said, "Because you asked me to stop calling you it."

At the time, I did not know the harm I had done. How could my "little" words have such a tremendous impact that they would change the course of life as I knew it? When reflecting back, I realized one thing: it was the start of my ego. The ego NEEDS power.

I felt the need to create an image for myself, one that led me further away from who I was instead of embracing who I am. When my mom stopped using my nickname, it was the first time I felt like I was the cause of something. This pattern continued through high school, as I was determined to create an image for myself while working from a blank canvas. However, while searching for an identity and picking up traits I saw on TV, in friends and relatives, etc., I inadvertently added layers upon layers from my true self, becoming self-conscious in the process rather than self-aware.

I briefly touched on how the ego influences our actions without going in depth to the impact it has on our lives. The ego has several layers that shape the person we become. The ego can be impacted by our family, friends, classmates and colleagues, and even more so, the environment we create. Once the ego evolves, it becomes difficult to unravel the layers we have built upon it until you identify what triggered the ego in the first place.

What Role Do You Play?

Would you be embarrassed if you wore the same pair of pants 5 days in a row? If someone calls you a name or says something disrespectful against you, do you feel obligated to defend your honor? If someone shows you the truth and you are proved mistaken, do you take offense to it? Are you defined by what you own? Do you measure accomplishment by the car you drive or the size of your home? Does your job define who you are? Do the certifications you own, or the awards you have won, say anything about who you are?

To break it down even further, what is your favorite movie? Who is your favorite character? The role an actor plays in a movie is not any different than the role you play every day. In a movie, the actor plays a specific character. The role is temporary during each take, so they do not become imprisoned by their character. You may not realize it, but YOU are a character. The role you play is the result of your ego. Your ego is not who you are, it is an image you created for yourself. You have become your avatar to create a sense of belonging to something or someone.

Most people believe that discovering their true identity is essential to their character and their path. This misconception is led by the current belief system. A person may be a victim of abuse, either in their home life or professional life. Most people are quick to put up a defense mechanism to protect themselves, so they develop an ego.

A person's ego gives them a sense of belonging to the roles they play in their daily lives. The role you play in your professional life often will cross paths with the role in your personal life. When your own life is affected, as the two roles conflict with each other, you may attempt to assimilate the two roles into one. It becomes easier to play one character versus two, so you continue to merge the two roles without noticing.

What Is Your identity?

As you attempt to discover who you are, you may find yourself inheriting roles from people you respect, including parents, teachers, friends, and even characters you see on TV. When your role evolves over time, it becomes an ongoing development and inevitably becomes an expectation of your character. Oftentimes, you become unaware of your ego, so you identify it as who you are. Having an ego means you are controlled by your image. When you are trying to protect your image, you have created a prison for yourself; it becomes hard to escape. You have this image you must adhere to in order to preserve the perception of you.

Putting your passion into something, whether it is your favorite sports team, politics, career, or family, becomes something you identify with as you feel it becomes a part of you. If something you strongly believe in is being attacked, your ego takes it personally, so you think and feel that it is YOU being attacked. You create an ego that is often used as a defense mechanism to protect your identity. As you continue to protect your identity over and over, it starts to become you.

When you find your work-life consuming most of your being, the effects of being on the Gravitron attract a new ego over time, and this becomes the new identity you associate most with. The more you become involved in your work-life, the more you feel the effects of the Gravitron, so you start to develop its habits. After generating the same pattern for 21 days, it becomes your lifestyle. After 90 days, it becomes ingrained in your character, and evolves further the longer you associate with your new character. The changes are ever so subtle, but can have a long-lasting effect that will alter the way your friends and family view you.

When you are at work, you are expected to play a specific role or character. Playing a role can be exhausting. After having various types of jobs, I found myself playing a new role. Each time, I found myself picking up a new trait as it became my sense of being, an identity to associate with.

You may have experienced this yourself, or from your parents after they come home from a long day of work, finding yourself mentally, emotionally, and physically drained. You associate it with what is expected from you, because it is what you need to do in order to provide for your family. You are expected to play a role 8 hours a day, 5 days a week. Anytime you are playing an uncomfortable role, being something you are not, it takes away from your energy. Putting on a mask takes effort and energy.

You often find yourself compared to others by your profession. Whether you are a musician, actor, doctor, teacher, custodian, food and beverage employee, etc., people often assume your profession defines your character. With this is mind, while you are taking on a role in your work-life, you become very protective of it, especially when it is not as glamorized as other jobs. You find yourself protecting your profession, especially when it isn't as high-profile as other professions, because you feel you are also protecting your livelihood and your persona. As you grow more concerned that your professional life represents your true nature, you develop a defensive role as if it defines your character. As you create these defense mechanisms over a long period of time, they become a part of your ego.

YOU Are Not Your Ego

My dad had a great profession working in one of the large automobile companies. He liked his job, but he loved the fact that it provided him with health benefits for his family, a pension, vacation, sick pay, and opportunities to pick up additional hours. He often faced scrutiny and harassment from acquaintances on his baseball team simply for not having the traditional white-collar job.

Like so many others, especially before the information age, my dad did not know how to balance his professional life and his personal life. He often found himself being ridiculed in his personal life as the person he was in his professional life. The people he associated with during extracurricular activities referred to him as a "factory rat." They called him "lazy," accused him of having "extended lunches," "arriving late," "leaving early," all as attacks for the "poor quality" of the vehicles when they would often break down. They felt he did not deserve a pension and all the other benefits that went along with being a "factory rat," to which he replied, "I'll get you an application." Of all the people he offered an application to, not a single person took him up on his offer.

My dad was constantly being attacked and abused for his profession. He perceived that any attack on his profession was an attack on his family, which his ego refused to allow. Over time, his ego evolved into defense mode, which led to bitterness against others' successes. He started to feel unworthy because of his profession, making it feel more and more like a job, rather than what its sole purpose was, which was to provide for what was most important to him, his family. He was attacked by friends, enemies, frenemies, etc. and created a shield of protection. His fear made him feel unworthy. His positive personality diminished over time and became negative, because he was acting out the reflection from others. His ego became a defense mechanism to protect his family and it absorbed the personalities he associated with.

As my dad continued to provide for his family, paying for my brother's and my college tuition, keeping food on the table, a nice home in the suburbs, owning a side business installing windows, he always felt the need to validate himself. He allowed other people's words to pierce his ego, which caused it to grow into a larger shell of protection. The more he felt the need to validate himself, the more paralyzed he became in his ego without realizing it. His ego took on a new life of its own as he became consumed with the validation of others, inevitably redefining his character. I always defined him as a disciplinarian. I later came to find it was all a reaction of his ego that he needed to create.

When I was a teenager, I remember reading my mom's yearbook and coming across my dad's comments. He wrote that the two of them were going to be the funniest couple ever. I laughed at this, because I only knew my dad as a disciplinarian. I did not see him having a good sense of humor. Then one day it made sense to me.

My dad's favorite television show was the *Andy Griffith Show*.

His favorite character was Barney Fife. He loved Barney's sarcasm and witty humor. Since the character trait was something my dad found joy in, he tried taking on the character trait as his own. He would attempt to use sarcasm as humor and a coping mechanism when he felt he was being attacked. His sarcasm over time developed into a sense of bitterness towards those who negatively affected him.

Accepting Control of the Ego

You cannot judge a person by how they act. You will never understand a person's actions without ever walking a day in their shoes. If someone behaves negatively, their experiences have been compiled day after day, month after month, and year after year, accumulating in their thought process. When a person builds negative thoughts in their head, they continue attracting negative thoughts. As the law of attraction states, thoughts become things. So, when a person is expecting something negative to happen to them, they are attracting more negativity into their life.

As a person continues to experience these defeats, they inevitably build a protective shell with their ego. Their reaction is from a compilation of built-up events, not an isolated incident. The most important thing to understand when it comes to someone's ego is that they have one goal in mind: protecting it. We can learn from their perspective so we can recognize what they are protecting.

There is no sense in arguing with someone if their viewpoint does not match yours. Simply try and understand their perspective instead of imposing your viewpoint on them. When you see the path from their perspective, you will realize their reaction is not a personal attack on you. You just happened to be there when the confrontation occurred. The outbreak was inevitable.

A person's ego can be the result of a traumatic experience during their childhood. Their ego may have developed to hide from a personal issue, a shield of defense from experiencing the same trauma again. As this traumatic experience passes, the ego subtly takes over, becoming the person they are today. The ego's defense mechanism is quietly planted in one's subconscious mind, and used to protect and shield off enemies who seek harm. Since it is planted deep in one's subconscious, the ego is unaware it exists, but continues to attract like beings in one's life.

The more narcissistic control and abuse you take in as a child and teenager, the more likely you are to comply with today's societal structure. Kids are taught to be followers. When they become young adults, they are expected to conform to people of higher rank without asking questions. When the same person assumes the same position, they become entitled to the same respect, as the pattern continues.

Do you want your kids to comply, or do you want them to become leaders? When inferiority is instilled in them, it becomes a weakness as they advance in their professional life. As the mind is being programmed as a conformist, the ego attracts similar beings in their professional life as well, because it is all the subconscious knows. For example, you can be bouncing around from employer to employer, and find yourself in the same situation you were in before by attracting many like-minded bosses. This is often why you hear "the grass isn't always greener on the other side of the fence," because you are attracting the same situation in your life. You are capable of shutting down as a common defense mechanism in order to comply with your employers' narcissistic tendencies.

Without knowing it, you become vulnerable and weak-minded, becoming the perfect prey for a narcissist. The cause of attracting people like this has been buried deep in your subconscious; it is the feeling of needing to be controlled by your boss/employer as it becomes your new natural feeling.

We were raised to obey, so we submit our power to higher entities, whether it be your parents, teachers, employers, government officials, doctors, etc. You have made compromises along the way because everything you are doing becomes an expectation, and that is to relinquish control over oneself and place it in the hands of others. When these higher entities continue feeding your ego as a form of validation to boost your morale, you accept what society has given you.

As you begin to reprogram your subconscious mind, you will see through various forms of control and manipulation. Behavior becomes predictable as it becomes similar across the board. When you become conscious of your situation, you will not allow yourself to become manipulated or deceived by the same person twice.

When you take a step back, and reflect on your experiences, all the pieces were there, and the event became predictable. The important thing to understand is to how to prevent something similar from happening again. The good news is that these experiences are building blocks to prepare your future you. Being a workhorse towards someone else's agenda may not serve your purpose the way it serves them. As you begin building your YOU, become thankful that the experience was temporary and you learned from a job. In form, it was small scale compared to building your empire where the effects become far greater in the grand scheme of things.

You Owe Me

A person's ego isn't strictly used as a form of protection. Ego is your character and varies from person to person. Some people have a humble ego, and others have a huge ego. Oftentimes, it is hard to rationalize with someone who has a big ego because they only view things from their perspective, which is a narcissistic personality trait. As the ego needs power and control, someone with a large ego will never accept the truth when conflicting views are present. They are close-minded to ideas that are not their own, and twist reality to fit their narrative. A person's ego will not remember each time you are right, but will be quick to point out the times you were wrong.

People who have a big ego feel entitled. Whether it is your manager, a parent, sibling, or friend, when they do something for you, they will make you feel like they are owed something in return. As Dr. Wayne Dyer states, "It would be like the Sun looking back at the Earth and saying 'You owe me.'" The ego cannot live without someone feeding into it. To protect yourself from someone's ego, do your best not to cater to it. The control-hungry ego will find new prey to feed off of.

I was guilty of having a big ego. My ego was an accumulation of who I was and my sense of being; the reason why I thought my wife loved me. I figured she viewed me as driven and a "go-getter." I did everything I could to protect it. I wanted to win awards, achieve certain titles, and continue to be recognized for achievements because it was who I felt I was and became my sense of being. I wanted to feel validated, so I strived for things which I thought were important to my wife and me.

When I was a teacher, I desired being teacher of the year and felt slighted when I was not even considered a finalist. When I switched over to the financial services industry, I found the industry was completely ego-driven. Everything was performance-based, as you would expect from a commission-driven sales industry. They had a large poster of company-sponsored trips based on achievements posted in the conference room. They posted agents' monthly earnings, sensationalized awards, and kept a running tally of agents' rankings on a monthly basis. I built my ego around the culture of the office. I set out to become agent of the month, selling the most life insurance policies in the office. I felt these goals would eventually translate into fulfillment, because it would include a higher earning potential and improve my social status, so I continued accumulating things that I thought would define me. The ego was all I had to define who I was and I felt that I needed to accumulate these achievements to become fulfilled and respected by my peers, wife, and family.

I found myself envious of those who won awards. I thought awards would define the person I was destined to become as I aspired to climb the corporate ladder. My goal was to be award-driven and conscientious of winning even more because it would lead to more income. After landing several school districts and increasing the case-rate within our office, my cases were not recognized at the same ratio for the agency's annual award ceremony. Even though the office's case-rate across the nation was 1:1, my ratio was 3:1. I felt that what I did for the company entitled me to additional perks within the office, which were never offered. Instead, they created a new category within the office for case-rate and basically ignored my contributions. It was a blow to my ego, but it helped serve the agency's agenda. It forced me to work harder so I could get the respect I felt I deserved. I later realized that I played into their system by trying to please a narcissist. One thing is certain, you will never please a narcissist.

I did not recognize my ego prior to working in financial services, and this industry exploited it even more. You were expected to compete with other agents and it glorified the ones who won these awards. If you were not one of the top-producing agents, you were perceived as worthless. By feeding into the egocentric methods of the managers, I further developed insecurities and questioned my value and self-worth. I thought to myself, how could one person from one company tell me what my value is?

My ego was developed in my subconscious mind without realizing it. I was taught to "be a man," and told how a real man must behave with their family, friends, and in their professional life. Reflecting on it now, I was attracting bosses similar to how my dad had raised me. I was drawn to authority figures who had tremendous egos, something I expected to learn from as I grew into manhood.

Recognize a Controlling Ego

There are a few personality traits that stand out in regards to a big ego. First, the need for power and control. Most things have to be their idea. Even if you have a golden idea, it will either get dismissed or will be spun into being their idea. Being right is more important than getting it right. When an egomaniac is found wrong, even when statistics are shown, it is either dismissed or turned into an argument, as it would appear to be an attack on their character or being.

The ego places greater value on accumulating material things than developing personal relationships. Cars, boats, watches, and a bigger home represent a higher rank in social status in the mind of one's ego to validate their self-worth. The ego will say, "if only I had this, I would become fulfilled." However, true happiness cannot be found from external validation and can only be found from within. If a larger house is what they desire, they will soon want a larger boat, and so on in an attempt to fill their empty void.

If a belief system is followed where image and self-worth are based on an accumulation of possessions, and family is merely background noise, then lack of awareness occurs, and the person becomes completely detached from consciousness. By placing value on material things, there is a disconnect from what is important. If an identity becomes lost in the ego, it may need to be shattered and lose everything to rediscover one's nature.

Having a strong ego spills over into your daily life and affects one's mindset. It is not something that can be turned off and on. New layers are added over time. It affects relationships, including business, friends, and your personal life. A person becomes conditioned to host an ego because it was what everyone was taught. While reflecting on your past, try and understand why relationships became sour time after time. Is it a pattern even after a change of social circles or change of environment altogether? When you notice a trend of negative experiences, you know that it is time to make a change.

If you feel you have a reputation or image of yourself to uphold, and are more concerned about what people think, you are not living for you. Your image, or character, becomes the foundation of your ego. The reason you continue to be trapped in the self-imposed prison you created for yourself is because you live in fear. Fear of what people think. Fear of rejection. Fear of who you are. Fear of change.

Erase the Ego

You will find the most toxic people are the ones who are controlled by their ego. These people will do whatever they can to protect it, even if it means harming you. These people come in all forms. They can be a boss, colleague, friend, and especially family members. A person who is controlled by their ego is unconscious to what really matters. Also, they either do not realize their ego exists or they assume everyone has an ego.

For those who are unconscious, the healing begins once the ego is broken. A person's ego can be shattered through a traumatic event, such as the loss of a loved one, a job, or when one becomes severely ill; in any event, one can experience a break from their ego when faced with their mortality. Once the shift from unconsciousness to consciousness begins, the ego can be released.

Removing the ego is a gradual process. Breaking free from your ego requires establishing new habits. Once the shift begins, you may experience yourself falling into old habits, but quickly adjusting to new ones as you become aware. Retraining your ego is not an overnight process. As you become aware of the work that is required, your ego will phase out slowly. As your ego diminishes, you start to feel comfortable in your own skin. Recognizing when you were wrong will not feel like a defeat. You will become open to newer, better ideas, and be grateful for being shown a better option that was not your own. You will no longer be influenced or affected by external factors that once stimulated you. Once the ego has diminished, the light that has been buried deep inside you will once again expose itself as it did when you were first born. This light will attract new people into your life, and new opportunities will open up. You will feel reborn as you no longer need to hold onto an image that separated you from yourself. The process will change your mindset, behavior, and it will inevitably change your life.

Breaking Through the Thick Shell of the Ego

A person's ego can be so strong, from years and years of developing it, that it becomes their only sense of identity. They feel it is something that truly defines who they are. Their ego has created this persona in their mind over such a long period that it becomes the path of least resistance. Their ego is their expected behavior, so they continue to battle for its protection. Breaking through the shell of the ego can be done when appropriately handled.

The first thing you can do is build trust with someone. The number one thing you can lose and rarely get back is someone's trust. You need to protect the trust you have in all relationships every day. The second you lose someone's trust, the relationship will fade, and it becomes even harder to regain someone's trust once again. It is possible, but very difficult.

The second thing to do is to try and understand their perspective. What caused them to think the way they do? Have they experienced any trauma in their childhood or early adult life? Understand how they feel others view them. Most people's perception of themselves is not the same as how others perceive them. You are your own worst critic.

To put this into greater context, off the top of your head, who do you think of? You probably think of loved ones, family, and a few of your close friends. That being said, how many people are thinking about you? Chances are, very few except the ones you are thinking about. However, you are still trapped in your own thoughts of how you think others perceive you. You should not care how others think about you because chances are you aren't even thinking about them. Someone who matters does not mind your YOU, and someone who minds, does not matter.

After you understand someone's perspective, you will be able to break into the shell of one's ego of who they truly are. You will witness their shoulders drop as if there is a newfound respect and trust with you, and a vulnerability which opens the door to their heart. When the shell cracks open, a light from their heart will shine through. The ego can become weakened over time, and the path that will lead you there is through the heart. Let them know there is no reason to validate themselves. When they have already proven their intent, their validation has always been supported with love.

Humble Your Ego

Every person is capable of learning anything they want. Just because you have not learned something yet does not make you stupid. You were simply unaware or ignorant of the topic. Therefore, do not let your ego prevent you from learning something you find interest in. Build on relationships with people who have similar interests as you.

People love talking about themselves. You preserve your relationship by having them teach you something you did not know. People like to feel useful, especially when they get to teach. This helps boost their morale, and they will feel good about themselves when serving you for the better. You can even learn a lot from their perspective by asking how and when they learned this particular information. You will understand their path and experience is slightly different than yours. This does not make them more intelligent than you, it just makes them more informed.

Knowledge is limited; imagination is infinite. Be humble about what you know; be curious about what you do not know. Insecurities are self-imposed. Do not be afraid to protect what you do not know. Not a single person has ever done anything alone. Thomas Edison, Nikola Tesla, Napoleon Hill, Steve Jobs, Elon Musk, and every other great received help along the way. When working towards a common goal, you will develop a mastermind between you and the group, coordinating in perfect harmony.

Allow your ego to learn from your mistakes. Embrace humility and accept that failure will be your greatest teacher. To learn from your experience, you need to accept reality for what it is. You can relate to these actions, whether in school, by an employer, a group of friends, or even your parents, that these actions take precedence over acceptance.

Remove Your Ego and Listen

As your ego weakens, you will begin to experience a lot more coincidences in life. Remember, there are no coincidences. Coincidences are when life happens for you, not against you. As Eckhart Tolle says,

> " The moment you become aware of the ego in you, it is strictly no longer the ego but just an old, conditioned mind pattern. "

"The moment you become aware of the ego in you, it is strictly no longer the ego but just an old, conditioned mind pattern. Ego implies unawareness. Awareness and ego cannot coexist."

If you force your way through an unsettling situation, due to stubbornness and lack of awareness of your ego, to "persevere" as one might say, then you will miss out on finding the right people to come into your life and discover your true passion. Instead, listen to the universe, do not quit, and pivot your intentions while redirecting your work ethic and determination into yourself, rather than for something less desirable.

The universe sends messages every day, either as reminders, or to redirect your way of thinking. You have to be mindful of the present. As the recent examples were drawn out over a long period of time, messages from the universe can appear more immediately. For example, you might be having a bad day, but then you get a message from someone very important to you that makes you immediately start feeling good. Another example might occur when you are writing about this very same chapter in this book, and your computer freezes and crashes without saving the previous content, so you end up having to rewrite the section in the chapter. Instead of dwelling on the mishap, use it as a sign from the universe to create an even better section in the chapter. The universe is a growing, breathing entity that will always work in your favor. Turning off your ego will enable you to respond appropriately to the messages that are being sent.

You have been conditioned on how to think since birth. Along with your parents, teachers, and religious instructors, your habits and persona were likely enhanced even more by friends, TV personalities, celebrities, etc. because you felt this need to connect with something to give you a greater sense of belonging. While you were being conditioned, you had this need to take on a persona in order to create an image or character of yourself. Your YOU has become your avatar that you acquired and created over time. When the universe sends you messages, your ego gets in the way of receiving those messages. Your ego can also desensitize your awareness of the messages the universe sends you. You can increase your awareness by being more present in the moment, inevitably weakening your ego and raising your intuitive nature in the process.

CHAPTER SEVEN

THE POWER OF THOUGHT

"The way our education system is structured, it will invariably lead to disturbed minds. A child is going from reading poetry to mathematics to chemistry. Everything is taught in disjointed ways because after all, no one is studying with a passion to know. Everyone is studying to pass the examination and get a job. This is a very destructive way of educating yourself and a pathetic way to live. But no matter how senseless it is, the majority of people in the world have chosen to live like that."—Sadhguru

Factory Conditions

Being a former schoolteacher with 10+ years of experience, I was able to gain a broad viewpoint of the current educational system. I taught in Michigan and South Carolina, with both using similar practices. The social structure does an adequate job teaching students how to collaborate, learn from various cultural and socioeconomic backgrounds, and develop quality organizational skills, to name a few. However, the schooling system does not prepare the kids for today's world.

Children are being programmed from birth on how to think based on their home environment, and this trend continues throughout grade school. Young children and teenagers are led to believe households are the same throughout the nation, whether they have a strict mother or father, family dinners, help with homework assignments or very little assistance at all. A child's morale lowers when they see another child receive something, such as a new bike or a new pair of shoes, that their own family cannot afford. However, the same student who just received a new pair of shoes might be envious of the other student because of their good grades, homemade lunches, and the love and support from their parents at home.

Students are not taught to learn another's perspective. Socially, they are taught to compare themselves to one another as if life is a competition. The intention is to believe every child is cut from the same cloth and are expected to perform equally and consistently with their peers. Anything less will be deemed as failure.

For the most part, students are taught to study the materials provided by simply memorizing information, only to regurgitate the same content back onto a standardized test. This is important to the students because their goal is to earn credits in order to move on to the next level of achievement. This is also important for the schools because federal and state funding are based on the number of students in the classroom and standardized test scores.

When I was in high school, an English teacher asked me what I thought on a particular topic. I said, "I don't know. You haven't told me what to think yet." It seemed rare to me to be asked anything that required thought. Independent thinking isn't common in today's curriculum and is rarely encouraged. The inability to teach students how to think for themselves has lasting effects as they enter adulthood. Life decisions are not merely multiple choice or true/false resolutions. Most adult choices require intense thought, which leads to fear of making the wrong decision, because adults have not been taught how to think for themselves or how to pivot from a bad decision. Unfortunately, the majority would rather have someone do the thinking for them.

Students are being programmed like robots and are expected to behave a certain way. The system encourages conforming within the structure society has built. By the time students graduate high school, most have the misconception they should already have their life goals planned out.

Many students develop goals and aspirations that are influenced by their parents or schoolteachers; most of which are misguided. When a student is undecided about their future, anxiety kicks in and they usually accept the first job that comes their way. Most students have this mentality of joining the workforce instilled in them with the universal life question at a young age, "What do you want to be when you grow up?" Students have this factory-like mentality because of the structure in place, including bells in schools that simulate factory conditions to signify transition.

The current model of the schooling system dates back to 1852, when Massachusetts was the first to adopt the state-sponsored compulsory schooling system. By the 1900s, all states had followed suit. The "factory model of schooling" includes:

- Standardization of teaching, testing, and learning rates
- Respect for authority over the exploration of truth
- Uniformity and orthodoxy over innovation and progress

The model in place does not stimulate free-thinking nor encourage personal growth. Students are not taught how to discover their purpose in life; therefore, many are unable to reach their true potential. As Ellwood Cubberley, states,

"Our schools are, in a sense, factories, in which the raw products (children) are to be shaped and fashioned into products to meet the various demands of life. The specifications for manufacturing come from the demands of twentieth-century civilization, and it is the business of the school to build its pupils according to the specifications laid down." (Public School Administration, Ellwood Cubberley)

The factory model of schooling leaves many lost upon graduation, and many enter college, trade school, or take a job, as if everything will start to fall into place.

After graduating from high school, you are expected to attend college or trade school to further develop your mind. You anticipate that selecting and moving forward in the field you wish to study will narrow down your professional focus. However, many may choose a field that has been suggested by someone they respect and trust.

Without proper direction heading into adulthood, you may seek wisdom from parents, teachers, and guidance counselors. You may find yourself respecting their opinion, since they had to make these same life decisions for themselves at some point. You assume they want what is best for you, and usually they do want what will be in your best interest, so you listen to them. You seek guidance because you feel what you choose today will be your livelihood for the rest of your life, so it needs to be something you can tolerate for the next 30+ years.

The Path to Misdirection

During school you might have glimpsed some subject matter that you were passionate about and found value in. Whether it be in the arts, botany, law, etc., there is a good chance you received a small taste of your desires, but never learned how to capitalize on it. Having to shift gears and switch classes often will lead to confusion as to what you should be pursuing once you graduate. Instead, the constant transition from one class to another, and the expectation of learning the required materials before you, creates an illusion as to what is important.

As we are programmed from point A to point B, we are taught what to think and what will bring value rather than discovering it for ourselves during our most fragile years of personal growth. Since we are following society's expectations, we then find a job with benefits and begin working our most able-bodied years, so we can start a retirement account and become independent and learn how to struggle paying bills.

Education will continue in your field of study. Whether you are working in the medical field, education, law, financial services, etc., you will be required to further your education and attend workshops within your company's agenda. Not only do you have to deal with the daily grind, you will have to put additional energy towards more education, oftentimes with required materials that do not provide further value.

These ceaseless acts of required studies will become something you must do as "part of the job," but that inevitably push you away from discovering your true purpose. Even if you are great at what you do, you will always feel unfulfilled if you are not pursuing something you are passionate about. To fully discover your true passion and potential, you need to ignore all the propaganda and begin listening to your heart. Doors will begin to open when you listen to your inner voice, which will propel you to begin thinking for yourself.

I found myself lost after graduating college, jumping from profession to profession, trying to fit in and become a cog in the system just like everyone else. I never had the flexibility to learn anything that felt fulfilling to me as a result of my work schedule. Between balancing a career as a schoolteacher, bartending at night, before being lured in and glamorized by the business in financial services, I was learning content that served the agenda of the company, and not myself; I was doing exactly what was expected of me.

Regardless of being in school or the career of your choice, you will be directed to serve another's agenda rather than your own. You end up putting all your energy into the meaningless content your company has provided in order to stay "sharp." This is also your company's practice to determine whether you will remain committed in years to come. After all, you are made to believe that having a career is something you are supposed to be doing and what you should be focusing your life around. Life becomes difficult because you are struggling to make a living rather than living your life, as you believe the narrative your company is selling you, and that is: if you continue to serve your company's agenda, you will be considered "successful."

After a long day, most people do not have the desire to discover their passion and feel that having a career is the antidote to merely "living the dream." As hard as someone worked to earn their current position, others will be envious of them and wish they could be in their position. We are told to not take our jobs for granted because we are easily replaceable. Therefore, we put our life into our work, looking over our shoulder every day as if we could be replaced at any given time. Unfortunately, employers will not tell us their job is just as replaceable. Employers should value you more than you value the job. If employers valued their employees as greatly as they expect you to value their job, you would see a rise in profit-sharing throughout the country.

At the end of the day, most people cater to the societal norms, unwind on the couch and drift away into a television series, before doing it all over again the next day. Most people think that "living the dream" through tolerance and annoyance is what you have to do to survive. The system currently in existence today will fail as human beings continue to evolve. When I was in grade school, I remember my math teacher telling us to learn basic math because you will not be able to carry a calculator wherever you go. Now there is one on every smart phone. Students are cramming useless information into their brains that can be found in a quick Google search. Technology is being created today that will change the way we use our brains (Neuralink). It is only a matter of time before companies use similar programs to replace you for their jobs.

Significance of Thoughts

"You are today where your thoughts have brought you; you will be tomorrow where your thoughts take you."—James Allen

Thoughts are the essence of life and your current situation. Everything you think of, whether it be positive or negative, will be played out in its proper form. When your thoughts are positive, you will feel bliss. Your positive thoughts will continue to elevate to new heights as you rise to a new level of awareness. You will feel the positive energy sit atop your head as if you are being lifted into the air like a helium balloon rises to the sky. You will feel this pressure encompassing your entire mind as if it wants your body to levitate. However, when your thoughts are negative, you have entered into a dark downward spiral as you continue to think of more things that aggravated you in your past. Every time you have a negative thought, the emotion will carry throughout your body and down your spine, lowering your frequency and pulling you to the ground. The energy from a negative thought is so powerful that you can feel it within your body like a dark cloud coming through you, causing your feet to tingle.

Your thoughts have been molded around you since birth. You were conditioned by your parents, schoolteachers, and religious instructors. The way you think is shaped by media outlets, friends, and people you work or go to school with. The people you associate with create a series of impressions as you are developing your ego. As you are picking up new habits through observations, your ego becomes the character you portray, a product of your thoughts and what you were made to believe was normal as you try to fit in with society. As your thought patterns repeat, particularly through association, your thoughts become your reality. You have the power to control your thoughts and create a reality in which you wish to live.

Your thoughts are continuously built into your subconscious, defining who you currently are, not what you want to be. 95% of the choices you make are controlled by your subconscious mind. When there is something you wish to change about yourself, you need to start from within to reflect the external YOU. As you extract your subconscious into your conscious world, it becomes the reality you experience.

If you want to make improvements to your current situation, change the way you think. You have the power to control your thoughts and how to respond if someone or something does not serve you. Your thoughts are more powerful than you ever imagined, and can be used to manifest the reality you desire. You are visualizing your reality into existence, whether you are thinking of it or speaking it aloud.

Listen to Your Voices

Do you ever notice when you are trying to sleep at night that your inner monologue is going crazy? It could range from replaying past events in your head to anticipating an outcome to a future event. These are all a distraction from the present. If it feels like your brain is actively going 100 mph while having the same conversation over and over again with yourself, you are not at peace in your mind. These are negative thought patterns, when your life is wrapped around speculation and hypothetical scenarios. Replaying events that have already happened or trying to anticipate an outcome from a negative experience clogs your mind, preventing growth. The ability to evolve is disabled when you allow something negative to dominate your thoughts rather than something positive.

When you free your mind from negative repetitive thoughts, doors open that can stimulate future growth. When your mind is clear, you allow dialogue from your inner voice, or higher self, to communicate with you. These messages will all be beneficial, such as how to engage in a certain relationship or job situation, a million-dollar idea, a new way to think, an inspiring quote that urges action, or responding a certain way to better your situation. If you do not take action from these thoughts, they may wither away or be passed on to someone else. Take the initiative by writing down your thoughts instead of saying to yourself, "I'll remember this tomorrow." By the next morning, as fast as the thought came in, it may be gone. These thoughts are coming from your higher self to guide you towards your purpose. To gain the most from these messages, you need to take proactive measures to retain them.

Write down your thoughts as soon as they happen. If you are traveling and do not have a pen and paper or computer handy, text them to a parent or a friend or write them in your "notes" on one of your phone apps, but you must remember to bring those thoughts to something you can always refer back to. I have made a mistake numerous times, texting someone a brilliant thought, only to forget to transfer it to another device that I can refer to. I sometimes had to go through hours and hours of texts to find certain thoughts before I taught myself to have something concrete that I can always go back to.

Where do these thoughts come from? Are your thoughts planted within your subconscious and becoming revealed as part of your natural self and true spirit? Are they sent to you by your higher self? Whatever the case may be, they are yours, and whatever you decide to do with them is up to you.

Negative Thoughts Lead to Negative Results

Every day you are given a choice. You can choose to have positive or negative thoughts. Your thoughts make up your reality. If you want to have a progressive lifestyle, then direct your thoughts towards the positive. Encourage those around you and become responsible for lifting spirits. A simple act of kindness goes a long way. Be thankful for what you already have, not what you do not have. By doing so, you will attract more positivity.

Have you ever noticed when something bad happens, something equally bad, or even worse, will follow it? Even when you try and change something, you continue to attract similar results. You may find yourself in a pattern of struggles that you cannot seem to get out of. It may seem like you are the victim of bad luck, and it just seems to follow you wherever you go. This is because your thoughts are continuously becoming your reality, so you are attracting negativity into your life.

For example, you may find yourself falling deeper and deeper into debt. Every time you think there is light at the end of the tunnel, something bad happens, and you attract more debt. Your car breaks down, your phone breaks, you need new appliances, the interest rate on your credit card increases, etc., and you find it harder and harder to get out of debt. As you take drastic measures by getting a second or third job, selling things from around the house, you are still repeating the same cycle, stuck on the Gravitron because your mindset has not changed. Since debt is at the forefront of your mind, you will continue attracting more debt. Every time you try and change something, the main focus is still debt. You have been planting debt into your subconscious mind, and debt is what you will attract. Without a sound plan in place, the more you work a job you dislike, the more you lower your frequency and vibration by remaining in the same field of energy that attracted debt in the first place. Eliminate the thoughts of being in debt from your mind and visualize yourself being in abundance. Repeat these affirmations over and over:

- -I am a money magnet.
- -I am abundance.
- -I am wealthy.
- -Everything I do turns to gold.

In the process, these messages will be sent out into the universe and harmonize your frequency and vibration to your thoughts into your subconscious, inevitably facilitating the universe to correct itself.

Negative thoughts about others only affect you. If you wish

harm on others, you are actuality wishing harm on yourself. Everything you say and how you react is a reflection of you! When you show signs of greed, envy, or jealousy, you lower your frequency in the process. This is a challenging world only if you allow it to become difficult. If you have this "dog eat dog" mentality, and feel everything is a competition between your neighbors, coworkers, friends, and family, you will find yourself in the same place for years and years until you change the way you think.

When you reflect on people of power, how many do you respect? Do you think people of power are happy? You have been taught in school that the most powerful countries use their power to control and influence others. Most identify with this as a means that the more power and control you have over others, the higher it elevates your socioeconomic status, which inevitably raises your frequency. Most believe that if you follow the trend large corporations and institutions have imposed on you and use it as a template, it will lead to happiness. This is not the case. Stepping over others for your own benefit attracts more negative energy, and you will never be happy. Your purpose is to serve others and do what you can to elevate their needs. Happiness comes from within and cannot be satisfied with material things or control over others.

When you are vibrating on a lower frequency, you will continue to attract events that lead to further misfortune. Even if you catch yourself making an honest mistake, the universe will expect you to correct the situation, even if no one is watching. If you have a negative experience, the universe will correct itself and respond equivalently to its action. For example, after grocery shopping and scanning all your items through self-checkout, you realize you overlooked something in your shopping cart. Once you get to your car, you realize the bananas were hidden behind a big water jug. Instead of going back into the store and paying for them, you compromise yourself by saying you will pay double next time. As you are backing out of your car space, you notice a lady next to you opening her car door. To prevent your side-view mirror from clipping her door, she is forced to quickly close her door. She screams obscenities at you. This confrontation could have been avoided altogether if you had gone back to the store and paid for the bananas. There are no coincidences. This immediate reaction, or instant karma, is the result of a negative occurrence. The universe will always keep you honest. Set your intentions to the highest form and it will raise your frequency every time.

No Need to Share Your Plans

When you are excited about a new idea, you may want to share the excitement with people you trust, respect, or love. You will find it is very difficult to have others fractionally as excited as you are regarding your ideas, regardless of how great the idea is. Too many times you will hear how impossible your idea is, which often leads to discouraging comments. "If your idea is so great, then why hasn't anyone ever done it before?" Too often, people will shut down your ideas time and again, as if you are waiting until one of your ideas will eventually "click" for them. The truth is, it will never "click" for them. When you start to notice people in your life continuously dispiriting your ideas, refract from them immediately.

Whether it be a romantic relationship, a parent, or a boss, often being told "no" on your thoughts can have a detrimental impact on your maturation process. In any relationship, when one person continues to give negative feedback, this behavior can be destructive, and is commonly associated with a narcissist. A narcissist can destroy your belief system, eventually causing your positive thoughts to become toxic. If you keep striving for someone's approval, you will never be happy. If you grow up in a household where you are constantly being discouraged, and nothing you do is ever good enough, it is a reflection of them, not you. Do not let someone's negative thoughts discourage you from becoming who you want to be. When you come up with these ideas, you understand the process that got you there. They do not. While seeking validation or approval for your efforts, know you can never please a narcissist. A narcissist is always gaslighting you and has to be in control of the dialogue, even when you feel they are appealing to your interests. There is usually a hidden agenda behind their approval and they will look for ways to steal your energy, even if they have to temporarily appeal to your interest when they sense you have been defeated. If the idea is not theirs, they will discourage you before making it appear as their own idea in another form.

Mute all negativity that surrounds you. People are negative for a reason. Whether it be insecurity or the need for power over you, people will continue to put you down when they feel you are rising above their status. There is no reason to involve yourself with them when it does not serve your purpose. When you determine that you will no longer grow and develop with someone who does not encourage your thoughts, or have your best interests at heart, stop engaging with them in the same capacity. If a parent says "no" to every idea, stop sharing your ideas with them. If an employer does not listen and likes control, remove yourself from the toxic environment; change jobs if you have to. The sooner you realize it is not you, it is them, the better off you will be and the quicker you will evolve into your natural form.

Your thoughts and your ideas are your own! You do not need to share them with anyone. You are doing more harm than good when you seek validation from those you love and respect. As your ideas continue to be shot down, over time you will become discouraged and lose your ambition before finding yourself conforming to society, eventually ending up as a cog in the system.

It is not that the people you love would purposely mislead you. They are simply expressing their limitations, not yours. They do not see the big picture as you see it. They cannot imagine what your thoughts and vision will lead to. They do not understand that each thought is a building block towards something bigger and greater as you continuously raise your frequency and vibration in the process. Do not let someone else's poor vision prevent you from being great. You are already great! You do not need validation from anyone.

Treat each idea as a science experiment, whether you are good in science or not. Basically, what it comes down to is trial and error to see what works and what does not work. You will learn what you can accomplish, and understand that your potential is limitless. You do not need to let anyone tell you what you are capable of. You do not know what you don't know unless you try.

You are capable of accomplishing anything you desire. Use the law of attraction as your guide: visualize what you want to achieve in life and see yourself as if you are already in possession of it. Not only do you have to see the plan, but you also have to feel it. What will it feel like once you achieve the pinnacle of your goal? Will you feel overjoyed with excitement? Will you feel overwhelmed with the attention you will receive? Once you have decided how you will feel, put the plan into action.

You Can Only Fill Your Shoes

Do not worry where you are in the journey when you begin to manifest your thoughts into your desires. It does not matter whether you have $1 in your pocket or $1 million. There are plenty of millionaires who are not happy. Money will not make you feel fulfilled, nor will it buy you happiness. Your perspective along your journey is specific for you. There is not a single person who has ever walked a day in your shoes except you. The life experiences you have encountered are unique to you and only you. Your maturation process from your environment developed the way you think today, different from anyone else, even if you are a twin.

Life is not a sprint once you decide what you wish to pursue. Many people are in such a hurry to get to the finish line that they forget to enjoy themselves during the journey. The journey is the best part of the process, so enjoy it! While you are putting your plan into action, absorb as much information as possible. Look for messages the universe is sending, and look at the big picture while conducting your plan of operation. You do not need to rush to prove your self-worth in order to receive validation from others. This will only lead to animosity and resentment when you reach your goal.

Think of yourself as a human pinball machine. As soon as someone responds negatively to your thoughts and ideas, retract immediately. Of course, you are welcome to be open-minded to other people's opinions, but do not let their negative attitudes be a deterrent to your beliefs. You have to learn on your own as if you are conducting a science experiment. Trust your gut feeling even if it goes against popular opinion. Surround yourself with positive people, even though it may be difficult out in public. Limit your engagement with those who complain about everything. Their attitudes are toxic, and it is how they get their energy. Just keep acting like a human pinball and bounce away until you are surrounded by people that are positive and make you feel good, those who are open-minded and support your thoughts and ideas. Do not concern yourself with those who are judging you. The people who are judging do not have the same experiences as you, so they cannot see from your perspective.

As you raise your awareness, you raise your frequency. The struggles you endured while in a low-frequency state resolve. Accept your actions for what they were, understand that the event no longer exists, and continue raising your frequency in the present. As you are raising your frequency, you will gain a new perspective. You may experience a lot of mixed emotions after raising your awareness. When you reach the moment of expanded consciousness, you will realize your past is not who you are, it is who you were. When that moment arrives, you will feel a break in your ego, relieving yourself from the burden you created for yourself. When you continue to raise your awareness, you will conclude that you have complete control over your actions, as your consciousness continues to shift. You are in control of you. Be conscious of how you think and act, because you are sending these messages out into the universe, and they will come back to you in another form. Similar to cause and effect, the more positive messages you send out into the universe, the more you will receive and attract positive results. You live in a constant "ocean of motion," and what you send it will reverberate back to you.

Think of your energy as if you are building a house. Every positive thought or action is equivalent to adding one brick to your house. Every negative thought or action is equivalent to taking away one brick. The more positive thoughts and actions you send out to the universe, the quicker and bigger you can build your house. Each brick will be similar to the "snowball effect" or compound interest in a financial investment account. The more positive you are, the quicker your results will compound towards your desires. The only question remains: How big do you want your house to be?

You will raise your frequency to a higher level, and soon the things you wanted will manifest into being. You will become happier because you are attracting positive things. If something terrible happens, control how you react and ask yourself and the universe why this happened and what can be learned or gained from this experience. You do the most amount of growing when persevering through adversity. Take the positive from each experience. Nothing is ever as bad as it seems unless you make it that way. Sit back and reflect. Watch your life unfold before you, as if you are standing over a chessboard watching the pieces move while planning the next move. You are in control of the moving parts, just make your next move!

What's the Hurry?

The greatest asset you have is time. It should be considered a valuable asset and should not be wasted on procrastination. Time is also the cheapest and most resourceful asset you can have when put to good use. Let everything come to you so it feels natural when it comes time to make a decision.

When I was about to graduate college, I had this sense of urgency that I needed to hurry and decide on a career, and I almost missed out on one of the biggest opportunities of my lifetime when I took on the role as Eminem's stand-in for *8 Mile*. For most people, time is abundant. You have your entire life to decide what you love to do. Be observant of your surroundings. Reflect and enjoy the journey of life. Ask yourself why certain people or events were brought into your life, only to leave as fast as they came in.

Nothing should feel forced. You do not need to hurry and graduate (or not graduate like Mark Zuckerberg or Bill Gates) so you can start your career. There will be plenty of opportunities waiting for you when you're ready. Experiment in a number of different fields to enhance your experience. If you do not love going into work every Monday and are experiencing a sense of resistance, find a new position. Float around as often as possible, and acquire new experiences. But what about money? Ask yourself, what do you need? You are able-bodied, you are intelligent, you can work ANY job to cover rent/mortgage. Food and beverage jobs are flexible and are always hiring. Would you rather be working a job you hate or doing something you enjoy?

Less than 5% of the population will ever achieve financial independence. Most people are financially illiterate while putting their trust into big banks and insurance companies, with the illusion that they are looking out for your best interest. By not understanding how financial investments work, the majority of the population will continue to work for money. As Warren Buffett stated, "If you don't know how to make money while you sleep, you will be working for the rest of your life." This is because we are not taught how to manage money and make money work for us.

Most people do not have a healthy savings account. They are lured by propaganda for material things they see in advertisements as something they must have. We have developed this keeping up with the Joneses mentality in order to seek fulfillment, so most people are taking everything they earn and throwing it into material possessions. Instead of teaching students how to work for money, teach students how they can bring value to other people. Money will follow.

If you want to have a successful business while achieving financial independence, think of something you are passionate about, which will serve a vast number of people. Do not go into business for consumerism. Go into a business that will serve other people's needs. Ask yourself, what are your plans with the profits? How can you reinvest your earnings into yourself and your business?

You begin to identify with those you most associate with. When you associate with millionaires, you assimilate with millionaires. Follow this mindset versus spending carelessly on consumer products. What benefits will you have when accumulating your fortune, and how can it be used for a greater cause while creating your legacy? What difference in the world can you and your business make?

When building your plan, write down daily goals. Identify what the big picture is when developing your plan. Strive towards your goal little by little each day, moving just a little closer to your vision. Put the action into motion, with the vision in place, becoming better the next day than you were the previous day, and your destination is inevitable. When you focus on your desires, with a solid plan in place, you will have the desired outcome as long as you know that nothing will stand in the way of achieving your goals.

Every person who has found their purpose has reasons for their achievements. Students should be taught to research people they admire and what motivations they had when pursuing their careers. The content should bring value to each child's life. Who do they admire and what influences inspired them? Students would have a broader perspective on life achievements by understanding their motives. They should focus their efforts and energy on content that will continue to bring inspiration and determination to their purpose by spending time in the classroom on content that resides in their hearts.

Creating Winning Habits

There are joyful people and miserable people. If you are in the habit of hanging around with miserable people, you will become entangled in their habits. Do not allow someone to control your emotions. Do not let them control how you think. Do not let someone's title entitle them to control you. When you allow someone to control you, you begin to view this as acceptable behavior, which will bleed into your personal life.

There is no need to control anyone. Everyone is the same. Any attempt to control comes from a narcissistic mindset and is a form of slavery. When a person's dominating thoughts are negative, it will spin off into further negativity.

Someone joyful will invite new ideas and will express compassion with you as well. A true thinker appreciates and respects the moment for its uniqueness. When you associate with free thinkers, it will allow you to keep expanding on your thoughts. When you become unafraid to ask questions, the more you know, the more you will question. You will find your true intentions when you question everything. You are an intelligent being with unique gifts. Having the right intentions will develop winning habits.

The habits you set for yourself today will be the same habits you will have throughout the rest of your life if you do not make a change. If you are clear on where you are heading and are happy, then enjoy the journey. If you are concerned about your future and it seems confusing and foggy, and you are not sure you are making the right decisions because something does not feel right, then consciously reevaluate your plan. You should always take assertive action.

Making a change in your daily habits can be quite simple. All it takes is a little bit of discipline, focus, and concentration. Write a journal of the daily habits you want to have. Whether you want to begin walking every day, practice yoga, meditate, become a writer, grow a garden, make your bed, become more organized, etc., write them on your list and make it a part of your daily tasks.

Begin your mornings on a positive note. As soon as you wake up, start your day by expressing gratitude. Find a "magic rock" and leave it by your bed as a reminder. After you wake up, grab the rock and say the things you are grateful for. You can say:

- Thank you for my comfortable bed
- Thank you for my health
- Thank you for my friends
- Thank you for bringing this person into my life
- Thank you for my yoga practice
- Thank you for my car

When you start your mornings off by expressing gratitude for what you have, more abundance will follow. The more grateful you are for what you already have, the more you will receive. Begin the habit of being grateful. When you start your day with a positive message, you have already begun your day on a higher frequency.

Learn from Experience

Personal life experience is your best teacher. If you never attempted it yourself or observed it firsthand, then it is just hearsay. Do not let someone tell you it cannot be done. They are simply telling you their limitations, not yours. I was told my limitations all the time, but this time I chose not to listen.

While working in the financial services industry, managers had a system of practices and procedures they wanted their agents to follow. Within their system, they emphasized that it was a "numbers game" and said to just blindly follow their plan since it had worked for them in years past. The managers glorified themselves about how well their system worked even though I seemed to have more questions than answers. I felt their system was outdated, so I developed experiences using my own tactics. I also studied other agents' procedures and used personal observations from their experiences to see what worked and what did not in order to help avoid many time-wasting activities. They continued to enforce these procedures for agents, which I was tactically able to avoid.

Financial service (i.e., life insurance salesman) was my first corporate and professional job after being a schoolteacher, and I wanted to position myself to make it a new career, even with the limited knowledge I had at the time. My obvious target audience was schoolteachers considering I was able to teach them something I wished I had learned when I was a teacher.

I was told it could not be done. I was told I could not break into the school system. I did not listen. I did not see anyone going after school districts, with another perk: voluntary payroll deduction. I was told it was even more impossible to have a payroll slot. Being a new agent, I should have believed them, right? I didn't. I had a hard time believing anyone unless I actually saw it for myself.

During my time in the industry, I landed over 10 school districts, enrolling hundreds of new clients, and brought new business into our office on an ongoing basis. I was able to use my resources to cherry-pick a team of agents willing to become part of the mastermind group. Having the right team in place enabled us to learn and grow together, even after our time in the industry has lapsed. We shared an experience and had fun working together, and still reach out to each other today as if no time has passed. When you connect with the right mastermind group, distance and time cannot separate the bond you have for each other and will always be an integral part of your ever-changing life.

The industry offered awards on a semi-annual basis. After achieving several awards and incentives, such as free trips to New Orleans, Nashville, and Dallas, the real value of the experience came from within. The external accolades were nice to an extent, but it was not the motivation that drove me.

I always had the desire to be an entrepreneur, and this industry was the closest thing I had to building a business without obtaining a business degree. More importantly, it taught me who I could trust and I learned to trust my intuition. Even when my feelings were off, it usually played out how I felt it would. This taught me to trust my instincts, but I had to get knocked down in order to get back up again.

Personal accomplishments through experience were far greater than what could be learned in the classroom. I learned how to build and run a small business through a lot of trial and error. I was able to improve public speaking skills while standing up and speaking to dozens, and sometimes hundreds, of faculty and staff members. I figured out how to pivot, accept rejection and failure over and over again, just so I could become victorious in the end. The accomplishments throughout the journey taught me to be humble from all the failures I had experienced.

Had I listened to the managers, I would have been nothing more than a cog in their system. When you become programmed to think like them, you lose a part of yourself in the process by not expressing free will. I was not going to let a few managers tell me what my limitations were. I knew my strengths and weaknesses and kept my head down and burrowed through. You know your strengths and weaknesses. If it does not feel right, and you feel like you're about to jump on the Gravitron, then it is not right.

You have to trust what you do and show sincere compassion behind it. I had the same compassion with school employees, as I knew the value I was bringing them. Being a former teacher, I understood the limitations school employees had because of their strict, rigorous schedule. I was able to seamlessly attend faculty meetings, prepare a quick 5-10-minute presentation, and shared the value I could bring them. I had school employees fill out a survey, and met with those who checked "yes." The majority were eager to learn, had the desire to learn, but did not know where to begin. Whether they purchased a product or not, I knew I was in the schools for the right reasons.

You do not need to set a goal just to prove someone wrong. Pursue the goal when it feels right. When you have the desire to achieve something, you have to experience it all on your own, whether it is success or defeat. It is not a failure if you do not accept it as such. It becomes a new lesson that teaches you. When you experience it firsthand, you will never have to worry about another "what if" scenario again.

Chapter Eight

ENERGY FLOWS WHERE ATTENTION GOES

People are energy. You are energy. Energy goes out. Energy comes in. Energy cannot be created or destroyed, it can only be transferred. In essence, there is positive and negative energy. How you use your energy can make the difference of feeling like you are on the Gravitron or not. Most are being used to serve another entity's agenda. Whether it be from a major company, a government program, or even a small business, your energy is being harnessed for their purpose. These businesses are compensating you for your time and energy. Your energy can also be stolen from you by people who do not have your best interest at heart, even when they are a family member, a loved one, or a friend. When you feel or observe being misled, deceived, and/or controlled, your energy is being transferred away from you; the effects of being on the Gravitron can last until you recognize the need to make a change.

Energy is contagious, whether it is positive or negative energy. As Newton's third law of motion indicates, "for every action, there is an equal and opposite reaction." What you give out, you will receive. Love is the greatest force (discussed in Chapter 11) you can give. You have the ability to spread your energy to affect those around you, whether it is positive or negative. What you attract is simply a reflection of yourself. If you want to invite more positivity into your life, surround yourself with things that will make you feel happy, encouraged, and inspired. Take the positive from your surroundings, and always look for opportunities to grow, while reflecting on your current situation.

You are much more sensitive to the energy in your environment than you ever imagined. When you feel really good about yourself, whether you just came home from the gym, enjoying a night out with friends, or spending time with your loved ones, your positive energy is a reflection of how you are feeling. You have the ability to absorb all forms of energy from your surroundings.

Negative energy has the opposite effect. When you send out negative emotions, you are lowering your frequency and vibration, and your energy becomes like a magnet. You will continue to attract negative situations into your life. Whether it be a pothole that blew out your tire, a traffic jam causing you to be late to work, or feeling miserable about yourself while having a few drinks at the local pub, you will continue to attract more negative energy. When you continue to surround yourself with toxic people who always find something to complain about, it becomes a part of you. Whether you realize it or not, you are feeding into their negativity and absorbing what they are giving out. You have become the audience for the complainers. When you decide to contribute to one's negative behavior, you are adding fuel to the fire they started. When you engage with a negative situation, you end up becoming sucked into their energy, which now becomes a part of your environment.

Do you ever notice when you are in a bad mood that you keep attracting more negative situations? You might start your morning by spilling coffee on your pants, then end up stuck in a traffic jam making you late for work, remembering once you arrived that you forgot your lunch at home, followed by your boss giving you a job assignment that is not what you are accustomed to, and the downward spiral continues. You notice this pattern continues throughout the day, so you say to yourself, "I should've just stayed in bed." We have all been there before! The events in your life are not a coincidence; they are a reflection of how you are feeling. When you are negative, you lower your frequency, affecting your vibration, attracting like energy into your field.

If you find yourself in an environment that appears toxic, while feeling a sense of discomfort, take a step back and reflect on your current situation. Process everything that is being presented and determine what can be learned from your experience. Slow down if you have to. If something can be learned, it will always be a positive experience. Sometimes, you just need these reminders, or wakeup calls, to shift your line of thinking in order to be directed towards your purpose. If you treat yourself as the victim, and continue to complain about your situation, chances are you will find yourself in the same situation over and over again because you have not found a way to grow from it, inevitably attracting more misery and becoming negative as the cycle repeats.

Like Attracts Like

You should not depend on others to serve your attention's needs. What you focus on at this very moment will have a ripple effect on how you think later in the day, tomorrow, next week, next month, etc. You cannot consciously multitask. Where you focus your attention, your energy shifts to what you are concentrating on. When you are continuously stimulating your mind with engaging content, you are raising your frequency and vibration.

Have you ever been on the phone with someone for over an hour, and realize you did not accomplish anything? Or when you watch a television show or series for a couple hours each night and realize you did not do anything to improve yourself or your situation? This world is full of distractions. Hours and hours of energy can be easily wasted each day, and you may not even realize it. If you are spending time watching a television program, engaging with someone where it is always "doom and gloom," or procrastinating, you are contributing to negative energy.

It is up to you to determine whether your conversation is helpful or destructive. In retrospect, the hours you spend engaging with someone may not benefit you directly, but instead, may benefit the person you are engaging with. When this occurs, you are serving your audience and taking on the healer role. When you are aware of your position, and understand your purpose for that person, potentially helping them refocus their attention for the greater good, you have served your purpose. For example, if you are having a conversation with a close friend over the phone, and all they are doing is complaining about their situation, they may be reaching out to you because they need your help or advice. Even if it feels like they are attacking you, your habits, or your way of thinking, they are only projecting onto you. No two situations are alike. You can either cater to their displeasure, or you can offer positive feedback or advice. You are responsible and in control of how *you* engage.

A Tale of Twin Brothers

My twin brother, Billy, and I were best friends, inseparable during our childhood. While many of our friends looked for best friends, I felt spoiled because I always had my best friend living with me. In middle school, I remember being at the mall one day, and saying to myself, "I can't imagine not having my twin brother in my life." We were a team. We did not have to call up one of our other friends to see if they could come over and play. We just did. We did everything together. We took on adventures, played sports, got into trouble, etc. Whenever we wanted to play a game of basketball, we would just simply ask. 99% of the time it was "Yes!" and we would just head out to the driveway and play a little one-on-one; even in our church clothes we could sneak in a game prior to attending.

One winter, Billy and I built an ice rink in our backyard so we could play hockey whenever we wanted. Even though we had so much fun playing that year, I did not want to build it again the following year because of how much I hated the cold, wet, and icy conditions. No matter how many layers of clothing I would put on, it felt like my hands and feet were going to fall off. At least when we played hockey we would work up a sweat, so I figured we would just use the ice rink at the local park.

The following year, I kept to my word and stayed inside. However, Billy was the king of determination to put the rink together, with or without me. He would say things to me like, "You're not going to play on it once it's finished." I would say, "That's fine. As long as I don't have to go out in the cold and do all that, then I don't want to."

I also knew he would get bored playing by himself and eventually invite me out to play one-on-one. After a month of putting the rink together, it was complete. He went outside to gloat on his success of completion and started skating around. After about 15 minutes, he caved and asked me to join, which of course I obliged.

We were very competitive with each other, but in a good way. We brought out the best in each other, while challenging ourselves at the same time. We fed off each other's energy. Billy and I were members of the Boy's and Girl's Club. It was literally one block away from our house. In the beginning, when we played sports, they made sure we were on separate teams. One year, Larry, the sports recreational coach, said we could be on the same team and we would just see how it played out. We were excited about this. Billy and I became unstoppable. We won our floor hockey and basketball championships year after year. I cannot be certain we won every championship every year, but it sure seemed like we did. During our last year of playing basketball, our club put the first ever "super team" together. We took all the best players in our club and competed in the first ever regional basketball tournament of Boy's and Girl's Clubs around the area. We won the championship, coached by my dad, the only regional championship our club ever won.

In middle school, we went to a basketball camp hosted by the University of Michigan. The entire camp was divided, and we were all on separate teams. Coincidentally, Billy's and my team reached the finals out of around 24 camp teams. My brother had really good ball-handling skills, and I was good at playing him on defense, and a better shooter from long range. My brother used his ball-handling skills to weave his way in and out of traffic to make his way to the basket and score. I stopped him 60-70% of the time. He argued, "He knows my moves" in a team tryout when playing one-on-one. I had a clear edge over him when we played one-on-one, but he was a lot better when it came to team basketball.

During the final match in camp, the coaches did not know our relationship. My coach wanted to win, so he left the starters in the game. The game was close all the way through. My teammates made comments, "We need to stop this guy." My brother was blowing through the lane, fearless, every time. I could have said, "He's my twin brother. And I know how to stop him." But instead, I said to myself, my brother is about to beat an entire team and coach, and there's nothing that I want to see more, especially once it became apparent I was not going in the game. As the game came down to the wire, Billy willed his team to victory: 21-19. I congratulated him as we were uniting at the end of the game. He asked if I was upset about my team losing. I said, "Heck no! I WANTED YOU TO WIN! They weren't going to play me. If they did, then I would've wanted to win." He said, "Oh, cool." Then I grabbed the plaque he'd just won, looked it over, handed it back to him, and thought to myself, "I'm not really missing much."

Our competition motivated us to become better, and it was inspiring and encouraging during the developmental stages of our life. However, we were unfortunate with how we were placed in school. During elementary school, aside from kindergarten and fourth grade, we were in separate classes. We did not understand why we were in different classes, but accepted it for what it was. Billy was learning something in his class, while I was learning something completely different in mine. We were not able to collaborate on anything we learned in school because the teachers were on different daily objectives. After quickly moving past our day at school, we continued our friendship and routine after school and maintained our competitive spirit with sports. By high school, the pattern began to shift.

Billy and I accepted that we were not going to be in the same classes, and we were not even playing the same sports in the fall. Billy played football and I ran cross-country. At this point, we both began to search for our own identity. It appeared our school was pulling us apart. We began living different lives and there was nothing we could do about it. We had already drifted apart by time football and cross-country season ended. The habits we developed in August/September had become our new system by the time basketball season started in November. Billy became the starter and I was the 12th man on the freshman basketball team. As his popularity rose, so did his ego. He began to let his ego take control of him, luring him to temptation.

Billy started hanging out with the older crowd, appearing more mature than he actually was. He began picking up different habits with his new friends, something I was not accustomed to. Usually, whenever one of us brought a new friend into our life, they automatically became both of our friends. When Billy brought in new friends, I was like, ok… these are our new friends now. It immediately felt uncomfortable to me. I thought maybe it was me who was not adapting to high school. His friends had cars, were growing facial hair, etc., while I was still playing video games and wanting to go trick-or-treating. Maybe it was time for me to grow up, I thought.

One night, after watching our school's varsity basketball team play, we were all leaving the packed gym. My brother had already assured me we had a ride home from the game, but were going out to eat first. I thought it was kind of neat to have a little extra fun with our new friends and was interested to see what the night would lead to since it was our first post-game experience. I can't remember if our team won or lost, but I remember the moment that altered our relationship, as I could see the energy begin to shift.

As we were packing into his friend's car, there was one more person than there were seats. This created a huge inconvenience for everyone in our group. Instead of taking everything in stride and arranging another source of transportation, my brother immediately turned to me and said in front of everyone, "Why don't you get your own friends!" I was in disbelief. I felt betrayed, shocked and heartbroken. My whole body went numb. I felt like my world was crumbling around me.

I had already felt our relationship drifting apart, but his comments devastated me, almost immediately severing our ties. He was right. I did not belong there and should not have been friends with them. They were *his* friends and *his* crowd. I was clearly an outcast, and the friendships did not feel natural. The energy of the group did not match mine, and soon, our relationship became strained.

Nothing around me felt right as I began searching for new friends. It was painful to see Billy being negatively influenced by his new friends, sinking into a black hole, falling deeper and deeper into a negative downward spiral. His negative energy was projecting over everything he did, creating an entirely new ego for himself. He argued when things did not go his way, like an entitlement. He was picking up bad habits, and began to lie and become deceitful. His negative energy shifted against me, and he began bullying me constantly. The brother I knew and loved was not there anymore.

Billy turned into a follower and began drinking, partying, and staying up late, while associating with people who stole, manipulated, and took advantage of people. Everything he was doing felt wrong and I could not figure out what to do to help. Whenever I tried to correct him, he would resort to intimidation, beat me up in front of his friends, or chase me out of our bedroom. Our relationship became strained to the point that I found myself grieving the loss of my brother as if he had moved to another country. He was no longer the same person and I was unable to entertain his negative energy to the point where I was forced to change bedrooms so I could sleep at night.

As Billy belonged to a new group of friends, I found myself in search of something positive, and brighter. I associated with acquaintances on the cross-country team, along with some classmates. I made sure I was around people that made me feel good, and was not critical of every move or decision I made. I was somewhat of a class clown during the first couple years of high school. It was one of my outlets in order to be seen, and I tried to use situational humor to feel accepted by my peers. I had a couple friends that I hung around with after school, but it never felt as authentic as what I had with my twin brother.

Finding a Best Friend

During freshman year gym class, there was one person I got along really well with – Mike. I did not think much of our friendship at first, assuming it would be just one of those friends you have in class which usually ended after the semester or school year. The main thing that attracted me to him was his free spirit and positive personality. He accepted everyone for who they were, and was nice to everyone. I found myself lucky to be acquainted with him. However, there was something peculiar with him. He was not caught up with trends to impress people he did not know, which I found refreshing.

The following year, Mike and I were reunited once again in gym class. He was a very good athlete and we were playfully competitive, especially in our new favorite gym sport – pickle ball. We used to challenge each other all the time, similar to the relationship I had with my brother. We had a lot in common. We both had a strict dad, and viewed the world quite similarly and had a similar mindset.

During the summer, we caught a Detroit Tigers baseball game. On our way to the game, we both knew there was a chance of getting a buy-one-get-one-free ticket marked under the cap of the cherry coke I had purchased. Without understanding the concept of the mastermind and manifesting thoughts, we had envisioned us winning a free ticket. We had imagined there being a free ticket marked under the cap. As we sat in anticipation of what would be revealed upon opening the pop bottle, we were discussing what we were going to do with the extra money with the free ticket. As I revealed the bottom of the cap, it read: Buy one, get one free! We were both ecstatic! Our thoughts had manifested into our reality, revealing our nerdish personalities in the process.

Our friendship grew stronger from there and we became best of friends. He was always a positive influence in my life and helped me make it through high school. Knowing what I know now, my thoughts attracted a person like him into my life because I was seeking someone positive. I was attracting what I became. Our energy, frequency, and vibration were aligned as if we were soul mates. Our friendship carried into college and into adulthood. Whatever obstacles and adversities we have been through, we have always known we could count on each other whenever we needed. Today, Mike is still my best friend, a bond that will never be broken. It does not matter how far apart we may be, our relationship will always pick up from where we left off.

Moldy Fruit Is Contagious

You know that image where a piece of moldy fruit is placed in a bowl with other fresh fruit? The fresh fruit becomes infected by the moldy fruit and the mold will continue to spread. Why doesn't the fresh fruit affect the moldy fruit to become fresh again? It is because the mold acts as an irreversible virus and contaminates the other fruit it comes in contact with. It does not have the ability to determine right from wrong. The moldy fruit is already contaminated and spreads and affects those around it. If you eliminate the infected fruit, you prevent the mold from spreading. The same goes with eliminating negative people from your life. You do not need to cater to negative people. You have the choice to ignore them and walk away. Once you sever ties with them, it will feel like a weight has been lifted off your chest. No one has the right to keep you from being happy. Whether it is your employer, family member, or friend, you are in control of who *you* allow to impact your life. You do not need to continue engaging with people who are not contributing to your growth and development. Your energy is valuable. Protect it like a king cobra protects its venom. It will not waste its venom on something it does not feel threatened by. Use your energy for good by shifting your energy to those who think similarly to you. As your energy evolves, you will see a shift in the way you receive information from the universe.

Anything you concentrate on will become a part of you and continue to grow. Whether it be positive (raising your frequency) or negative (lowering your frequency), it becomes attached to you. You have control over what enters your mind. When you engage with something you find stimulating, you are growing towards your greater purpose. Your energy will be drawn to higher frequencies. You will compound your gains each time as you reach new heights. Your setbacks will become your old highs. As you keep elevating your energy to a higher frequency and vibration, you will attract what you are searching for much faster than anticipated. You will find new, unimaginable experiences manifesting. You will observe the linear trend and draw connections with what has been established. You will be able to visualize new realities being manifested as you are closing in on your desires. Every time you learn something new, your brain is making connections, as the universe is correcting itself to match your frequency from repetitive behaviors.

Your expectations will evolve, along with the desires you wish to manifest. The more aware you are, the more sensitive you will become to different forms of energy from your surroundings. Your intuitive nature will grow stronger. Your experiences will become greater, with each being a step towards your true purpose. New experiences will lead to new opportunities. You will not be able to visualize everything at once, but as you progress along your journey, doors will open, physically and spiritually. As you walk through these doors, you will begin to visualize more of what lies ahead as you continue your journey through the next door. The more aware you become of your surroundings, the quicker and easier it becomes to pivot around forthcoming obstacles.

Feed Your Mind, and the Rest Will Follow

The people you associate with have a significant impact on your reality. You might find yourself in a situation where you are completely exhausted after being around them or you might find yourself being uplifted. Whatever the case may be, you will adapt to what fits your needs. You have control over your mind of what you want to become reality. Stop looking at the past; the past does not exist. When you keep focusing your energy on the past, your future will be a repeat of your past. See yourself in the future. Who is the future you? What does the future you like to do? What does the future you aspire to be? Visualize yourself being that person every day until it exists. Meditate daily and visualize your future.

What does it mean to lose your ego? Losing one's ego means you have raised your awareness from your image to who you are, in search of your greater purpose. You have become awakened. As Eckhart Tolle states, "Awakening is a shift in consciousness in which thinking and awareness separate." As you experience a shift in consciousness, you get in touch with energy. You will be able to anticipate someone's actions, emotions, and intent as they have not separated themselves from their ego. Being in touch with your emotions, and learning how to control your energy for every situation, means you can observe the energy field around you. You can sense how to respond based on the current frequency of the room. Every action requires energy. Wherever your thoughts go, energy is being used to direct them. When you begin reading energy, you will be able to bounce around like a pinball from one form of energy to another, gravitating towards your purpose.

Energy is transferable from one person to another, and comes in all shapes and forms. Like the mold on the fruit, people became infected by toxic personalities and negative forms of energy, which then become a part of them. The more consumed you are with negativity, the more difficult it is to overcome. Associating with positive people can have a significant impact on your well-being.

Being positive can be difficult, when you allow it to be. When life becomes challenging, you have already made up your mind that it is difficult to be positive, especially when battling through adversity, temporary failure, and unavoidable growing pains. You need to dig deep down and find yourself in these situations. You have control over how you feel, so look up at the universe and ask what can be gained from a negative experience. Learn how to turn a negative situation into a positive one. You cannot control what happens, but you have complete control over how you respond. 100% of failure is an illusion trapped in your own mind. What separates failure from being great is what you want to get out of life.

There are several things you can do for yourself in an effort to find your true purpose, and bring more positive energy into your life. First, turn off the television, especially news and media outlets. Television is known for "telling lies to your vision." You are made to believe everything you are watching is your reality, and the majority of the news out there is negative. If you find yourself inundated with negative news coverage, or even shows that have a lot of violence, you begin to accept the negativity as part of your reality. Nothing is allowed in your world unless you let it in. Most importantly, do not fall asleep with the television on. Even though you are asleep, your subconscious is recording everything 24/7.

One of my favorite things to do is go for long walks in nature, and listen to an audiobook with enlightening content to stimulate my mind. This helps clear my head and prevents toxic thoughts from entering my mind, and also helps me become connected with nature and being in the present moment. The more connected you become with yourself and nature, the more refreshing your life becomes. Science has proven that being outdoors in nature reduces stress and anxiety levels, and helps you feel rejuvenated. To amplify your reset button, stand on the ground in your bare feet. This technique is called grounding, electrically connecting you to the Earth. You do not need to be around anything extravagant in order to practice grounding. Simply stand outside on the ground (no pavement of any kind), and connect the soles of your feet to the ground below for a minimum of 5 minutes. Try doing this every day. It is very helpful when you have a migraine or when you are not feeling well.

Always demonstrate gratitude. The more positive you are with what you have, including people in your life, the more you will attract more positive energy. Avoid being negative at all costs. When something bad happens, look for the silver lining. Reflect on the event, and ask the universe what was learned from this experience. Understand how the experience will help you learn and grow mentally and spiritually. Instead of dwelling on something bad that has happened, always take it as an experience you can grow from. Your future self will thank you.

Working out, eating right, meditation, getting enough rest, and positive self-talk are a few more ways to bring positive energy into your life. Try to acclimate yourself to being positive on a consistent basis and make it your daily habit. Establish a pattern for yourself of being positive that will continue to evolve as you become more enlightened. You will find yourself attracting more like-minded people in your life by simply changing the way you think. This positive energy grows in your subconscious, and will continue to attract more and more positivity in your life.

Attracting positive energy and surrounding yourself with positive people can have a significant impact on the rest of your life. You will soon discover that attracting more positive people will lead to further advancements in discovering your true purpose and identity. While my brother and I went our separate ways in high school, it had a substantial impact on our different journeys that followed. Even though we are twins, the patterns we set for ourselves were the result of the people we associated with.

CHAPTER NINE

FORGIVE

Humans are the only life form on this planet that are punished for the same mistake over and over again. Unlike the rest of nature, we have this inability to let go of our past and also have other entities reminding us of our mistakes. We keep reliving the same events in our minds as if we are stuck in repeat mode. Living in the present can put your mind at ease, but in order to do so we must be willing to express forgiveness.

Forgiveness can be found in two forms. First, forgiving others. This can be found in many forms, but it is either for their actions against you or against someone else that affects the way you view them as a person. Second, forgiving yourself. This can be from something you did or experienced many years prior that became a hurdle in your life, especially when it is absorbed in your subconscious as the way you think. This mental barrier becomes an obstacle which you have allowed to condition you as the person you are today. You may find that you are imprisoning yourself because you should have known better. Instead of forgiving yourself and moving on, it snowballs into a deep, dark depression that you accept that you will have to cope with for the rest of your life. Either one of these forms of forgiveness will set you free from control. Control is a mindset that has been placed on you and has a profound impact on how you progress in life when you are not willing to forgive.

In order to forgive someone, you have already condemned them for their actions instead of accepting them for who they are. Oftentimes when you hear the word "forgiveness," you associate it with someone who has done you wrong. Most people find it very hard to forgive someone for their actions against you because they have committed an offense without taking your feelings into consideration. This means you held someone to higher expectations who does not necessarily hold the same standards for themselves. When you allow someone to penetrate into your thought process, you continue to blame yourself for allowing them get to you.

Forgiving Others

The most sound and sincere asset we can have is the ability to forgive someone. The people we usually have a hard time forgiving are the ones who are closest to us and who we feel are preventing us from expanding. Whether it be a parent, loved one, sibling, friend, boss or colleague, we may often place too much emphasis on how we think they should act towards us. If they fail to meet some certain criteria, we might begin to feel helpless or that we are not good enough.

For example, it can be something subtle, like "What do you think of my garden?" Instead of a compliment you were expecting, you might get a response like, "Did you buy the right kind of dirt?" In this scenario, you were expecting a compliment. However, you were given unsolicited feedback without acknowledgment of your hard work.

Someone's negative actions against you, whether it be physical or verbal, leaves you to question what you did to deserve this sort of mistreatment. As we continue having these dominating thoughts, we continue attracting more of these occurrences in our relationships because it is largely ingrained in our subconscious and it is the behavior we are expecting to receive.

We might shift the blame and say, "Why should I forgive them for their actions if the same actions continue?" We might also say,

"Why would I forgive myself for them when they are the ones inflicting pain onto me?" When you forgive someone, you are not exonerating them for their actions against you. You are freeing yourself from their control. Forgiveness goes a lot deeper than saying you forgive someone. Forgiveness is something you have to feel deep inside of you. You must understand that their actions are a reflection of them and how they were programmed to think. You could show compassion and empathy towards them because they do not know any better.

You might find it more difficult to forgive someone especially when you allowed the abuse to go on. At the time, the abuse may not seem like a choice, as it becomes more about survival, so you accept it for what it is until you can leave your situation. Even if the abuse, whether it be from a parent or loved one, has gone on for several years, you can still find peace within yourself once you allow yourself to forgive.

Forgiveness does not need to be said verbally to the person you are forgiving. It is telling yourself that it is okay to have allowed it to go on for so long and that you are willing to let go of any trauma you have been holding on to. Remind yourself of the following:

1)   It is not your fault.
2)   It is a reflection of them, not you.
3)   You did what you had to in order to survive.
4)   You took on the burden of their control because you love them.
5)   It is only temporary.
6)   You love the other members in your family, so you are willing to sacrifice yourself for their freedom.
7)   You've dealt with this before, so what is one more time?
8)   Have empathy for them because it is how they were taught to think and they do not know any better.

You might not realize harm is occurring to your well-being. Many years later, as you reflect back on your life, you suddenly remember why you are the way you are, and can often pinpoint a certain repeating occurrence from someone close to you. You might start by saying to yourself, "If only he hadn't pressured me on everything I did in my childhood, then I'd be a lot more assertive at taking risks. It's his fault that I am like this." Once you realize this pattern was established early on in your life, which had a negative impact on who you are today, you might start resenting that person. When you resent someone, you are attracting more negativity in your life, so you must forgive.

You may find it very difficult to forgive. Forgiving someone is one of the most difficult things you can do for yourself. When you forgive someone, you are, in actuality, forgiving yourself for allowing yourself to be under the control of someone else. You are not exonerating the person for how they mistreated you. When you forgive yourself from that person's control, you are freeing your mind by no longer allowing yourself to be under the hypnosis of someone's spell. Because you can forgive yourself, you will become a better, more vibrant person from this experience. You know that you have the rest of your life ahead of you. You know you will no longer allow yourself to become susceptible to this kind of abuse again and will become more aware and stronger because of it.

What kind of advice would you give someone who is the same age as your younger self suffering from the same abuse? You will want what's best for them because they are a reflection of the current you. You became the person you are today because of the patterns you established for yourself at a young age. The pattern of your thoughts, beliefs, perception, how you are supposed to act, and how you were conditioned are all behaviors that you accepted as your own. Your current belief system is an accumulation of everyone you were associated with.

As it only takes a small part of your life to develop new habits and make them your lifestyle, the same patterns you have set for yourself are similar to being in a hypnotic trance for years while you were just going with the flow. You have already been programmed for years, and now it is time to reprogram your previous beliefs into new ones. The goal is to take the advice you gave to your younger self and unravel the knot in your brain from the spell. Tell your younger self that this belief is not you, it is someone else. Slowly but surely, you will begin to unravel the knot tied up inside you. Only this time, you will be conscious of your habits, and they will become your lifestyle.

Do Not Live through Someone Else's Agenda

Being unaware of mistreatment and abuse is very common. You accept it as your reality without realizing the long-term effects it has over you. Abuse can be something subtle in the household, from a sibling, a classmate, a teacher, a religious instructor, etc. as a form of bullying. When you accept bullying as your reality, you become closed off, building a shield around your ego. If you live in a household where you see conflicting behaviors, seek the light that makes you feel empowered. If you cannot find it inside the home, seek it elsewhere, and just know, your current situation is only temporary.

Assume you have one parent who makes you feel strong, and another who makes you feel weak. Their behavior is only a reflection of them. What you allow into your life is up to you. For example, if your mother made you feel as if you could accomplish anything in this world, but your dad made you feel inferior and weak, ignore the negative behavior, and seek the positive. If you are being pressured, controlled, and insulted regularly, stop seeking their approval. You will never please a narcissist. If you find that trying to please someone becomes work, and they make you feel every idea you have is bad, or you are not worthy of their time, stop trying to earn their approval. When doing so, you are shutting yourself down, and conditioning yourself not to express further passion for what you are trying to accomplish since you experience defeat after defeat. As it comes to your schooling, career choice, or even the car you drive, you seek approval from the personality you find most difficult to appeal to. While you are looking for their approval, you begin to listen to them as they dictate your path that will make them happy, not you.

When this trend continues, you seek a career path they have suggested for you, steadily gaining their approval. It feels like a minor victory for you. Since this family member strongly believes that your title (doctor, teacher, lawyer, etc.) defines who you are, you listen since you do not know any better. As you become the person that they wanted you to be, you realize it is not what you wanted to be. At some point, you realize they are trying to live through you. Upon this discovery, you become resentful, bitter, or angry. These are simple emotions to feel, but should not be held onto with regret. As you become aware, look at the positive in every situation. Now you know what you do not want to be, so now you can become the person you always desired, before external forces influenced your perception. You are now in control of your life, so follow the path of least resistance – what feels natural to you.

Forgiveness Eliminates Control

My dad was a strict parent when I was growing up. I was scolded for my mistakes, and some measure he took I felt were a bit extreme. I didn't think anything of it at the time. Little did I know I was being conditioned to behave a certain way to mirror the person he desired me to be, not who I wanted to be. My personality seemed to deteriorate the more lost I became with my innerself.

Then one day, I had an awakening of who I'd become from who I was. This epiphany came over me like I was spinning around on the Gravitron before it suddenly came to a halt. The bitterness and resentment I had for my dad was something I'd never felt before. For the next 13 months I slowly remembered the different ways I'd been disciplined, unraveling layers from my ego in the process. Each layer that was removed was a layer of an insecurity I did not know I had developed over time. These insecurities were like having a curse hanging over me. Little by little, as I kept remembering things, I called my mom up to tell her what happened when I was younger. She was quick to tell my dad, which deeply hurt him. My intent was not to cause him any pain. However, as my bitterness grew, he suddenly became ill. He was sick for a couple months and did not know if he was going to make it. He said, "I'm being punished because of how I raised Tony."

I did not want my dad to suffer. He has always been a strong person and rarely got sick. Even though he was very strict with me, he was always the first person to have my back whenever I needed his support. He did his best to support his family, and I knew that.

Then one day, after hearing how sick he'd become, I wanted to see him healthy again, especially so we could work on our relationship. I thought to myself how the strength of his words had negatively impacted me and that the strength of my words was negatively impacting him. I called my mom and said, "Tell Dad I forgive him.

Tell him I'm not mad anymore." Even though, at the time, it was a lie, I needed him to think I had forgiven him so he could get better.

That weekend, as I was quietly sitting on my couch, I felt an energy of forgiveness shift through me. Suddenly, I forgave my dad. I realized that it was not his fault how he treated me. He was raising me by how he was raised. He was never taught how to deal with adversity, so he added layers upon layers of bitterness and resentment that became his ego. I forgave him. When this happened, I had this feeling of weightlessness of control that I'd never felt before. I had peace of mind, and I began to see myself evolve from there. In less than a week, my dad's illness was healed, and it felt like both of our curses had been lifted. I am forever grateful for the experience and love my dad even more today than I ever had before.

Two things can happen when you are sending forgiveness out into the universe: 1) the person you are forgiving might suddenly become healed from an illness they are experiencing, 2) a sudden sense of weightlessness will come over you. You may be overcome with emotion or overjoyed with a peace of mind that you are no longer under their control. After speaking the words aloud to the universe and into existence, you are making a contract with yourself that you are willing to surrender being controlled. By making the agreement, you can expect a time delay when the actual feeling of forgiveness takes place. It may take less than a week, a few weeks, or even a few months. Repeat the affirmation over and over when it is necessary. Only YOU know what is best for you.

By forgiving them, you suddenly regain control of your life. You will no longer feel the need to blame others for your misfortunes. You will know that this experience will continue to help you grow and evolve into the person you desire to be. Once the forgiveness takes effect, you will find that you have zero trace of bitterness and resentment in your mind. As a result, the negative people you have attracted into your life will soon dissipate, and you will repel them. You will become grateful for the experience you had because now you will no longer allow yourself to be manipulated or controlled ever again. You will show gratitude for the experience because it will protect you from being vulnerable and manipulated later in life.

Forgiveness Becomes Freedom of Control

We have been raised in a system of control, and we may not be fully aware of our vulnerabilities. We have been conditioned since birth for our current belief system. We accept the belief system because it is all we know. It is our culture. As you become conscious of the decisions you make, the seed in your unconscious mind becomes susceptible to manipulation, and accepts forms of control.

We have been conditioned since birth to think a certain way and follow people who have a similar mindset. Some inherit the role of control because it is what they have grown accustomed to based on their role in society. The role they play is an extension of their ego that they perceive as real, and the need to impose their will is defined by their role. Because of conditioning, you have accepted that there needs to be a sense of give and take in any relationship. In most cases, you hand over control to authority figures.

Forgiving someone for how they mistreated you does not absolve the person for their abuse. Most of the time, they have their own battles they are struggling with. Most people who feel the need to control you do not realize they are controlling. They are merely following through on their beliefs and what they have been programmed to do. They cannot be told where they are lacking, they need to discover it themselves. They are imprisoned in their own minds, with the need to protect their self-imposed, self-created image of themselves: their ego.

A person's ego can have a detrimental impact on their life. As they try to protect a character they portray, they becoming further lost in the system. They know not what they do as it becomes an expectation of their character. All of their experiences up until this point have been through a lens that 98% of the population falls victim to.

Forgiveness does not happen overnight. It is a process. A person's actions can be forgiven in the moment, but how a person feels about you after those actions may take a lot longer to forgive, especially when the impact was lasting. After discovering the cause of someone's actions against you, you may begin to feel resentment towards this person. You may trace their behavior back to where it originated, and blame them for planting these false beliefs in your head, creating a pattern of life events that affected the position you are in today. The power of forgiveness not only removes someone's control over you, but it also eliminates control over yourself!

CHAPTER TEN

ENVIRONMENT

You grew up in an environment that is entirely different from some-one who lives on the other side of the country. Your environment is also different than your neighbor's. To extend it even further, your environment is as different to you as it is for your own sibling, even though you grew up in the same household. Not a single person comes from the same background as you. You are unique in your dimension. Your physical surroundings, religious and spiritual expo-sure, and how you process and interpret information in your men-tal state are all factors that influence your environment. How you respond to your environment creates unique conditioning for you. As you adjust and pivot from your current surroundings, you begin the process of changing direction towards the trend that has started. This becomes your flow. Through habit, the repetitive patterns will act in a constant flow state that will project your life as if you jumped on the Gravitron. Always evaluate your current situation and reflect whether the trend you are making today will benefit your future self.

I grew up in a household with an older sister, twin brother, lov-ing mother, and a strict father. It seemed like the norm for every household across America. Everyone had a role to play, similar to the stereotypical families on every television show, so it became an expectation. Was it stereotypical, or was it something I was attracting into my life based on my current belief system?

Your environment influences your thought patterns. Who you associate with should be as conscious of a choice as your nutrition. What you feed your mind impacts what you invite into your life, inevitably affecting your environment. You may notice you are attracting similar experiences from people who enter and leave your life. You are attracting these people into your life through the repetition of patterned behaviors. If you find yourself in an environment where you are surrounded by negative people and deferring to gossip, you might find yourself joining in the gossip as well so that you can be a part of something. If you want to attract positive people in your life, begin by becoming the change you seek. Soon, friendlier and more positive people will enter your life and the environment you seek will become more positive.

Are You a Product of Your Environment?

Whether you are a victim or a victor of your environment is entirely up to you. LeBron James stated that a kid like him, growing up without a dad, raised by a single mother, to achieve what he has accomplished, is inspiring for kids with a similar upbringing. However, a kid may have a similar childhood, except they may have both parents in their life. Instead, their father is a narcissist who finds failure in everything they do. After constantly being told they are not good enough, they end up closing themselves off before completely shutting down. The kid is made to believe they are a failure because they should have an edge by having both parents in their life. If they had not had a father in their life, they might have viewed the world differently, because they would not have had a belief system that made them feel inferior. What we define as normal does not mean normal for anyone else.

You begin your life by studying human behavior to determine what you view as normal. You start by imitating your parents, siblings, what you see on TV, classmates, religious instructors, church attendees, social gatherings, etc. You observe the responses and reactions from those you respect the most, and question the behaviors that do not fit your structure. At a young age, you determine your environment has become your version of an acceptable form of behavior.

What you view as acceptable is created from a system of beliefs imposed on you, starting with your childhood. If you come from a household where cursing is allowed, and enter a home where cursing is not allowed, you will be perceived as a bad person because of your choice of language. It does not mean you are a bad person. It simply means the views from your environment are different.

Your school system continues to teach you forms of accepted behavior as an extension of what you should be learning in your home, mostly to accept control and expect to conform and abide by systems already in place. The teacher's classroom rules and procedures become identified as an expected form of behavior. Since the school is teaching you about structure, you place as much value on the social structure of the school as you do on your own home. Students become friends because they have a similar structure in their homes. They continue attracting similar students who have a similar upbringing because it is what they identify as normal. You associate everything you learn in school, on the playground, your views on the curriculum, and interactions with the teacher as good or bad. What is considered good or bad comes from perspective of a given environment. A "B" in math might be considered good for one student; however, it could mean punishment and require a math tutor for another student. These can all be acceptable forms of behavior based on a person's environment.

Recognize a Toxic Workplace

I have worked in a lot of great environments during this journey. Employers who take care of their employees stand out more than the employers who take their employees for granted. Regardless of profession and job description, everyone deserves respect. If you find you are working in a toxic work environment, you do not owe it to your employer to stay with them. You owe it to yourself to find an employer who will treat you the way you deserve to be treated.

Food and beverage (F&B) can be fun, but it can also be

long-lasting! Once you start working in F&B, make sure to experience as many restaurants as possible. Do not stay in for the long haul or it will grind at you. Sure, memorizing a new menu is not fun, but after going over and over it a thousand times, you will be glad it is something different. While you are in the industry, make sure it is temporary. Set your sights on your purpose and use F&B as a pivot point for taking that next step.

Many managers in the industry are friendly, but there are several who are controlling. Many times, managers feel they can speak down to you because they are the manager and you are the employee. If you do not want to get fired, you listen and obey because you have to. These managers command respect, but do not feel the need to give respect. Most employees bite their tongue, but later share with fellow employees how the manager mistreated them. Then an employee empathizes with the employee who had a different issue, or something equally as bad, creating friction amongst employees and managers throughout the workplace. This can lead to low morale.

Being older than many of the managers and having more experience than them, I decided to set bartending aside and work up close with everyone in the kitchen as an expediter. I worked alongside a 17-year-old high school student, Trevor, who was basically teaching me the system. These managers had the most toxic behaviors of any restaurant I had ever been in. During the downtime, I found myself mentoring him, making him aware all restaurant environments were not like this. We were surrounded by vulgarity, and everyone accepted it as part of the job.

One situation in particular really stood out to me. Trevor and I were working alongside the managers on the line, assisting in getting the food out of the window as fast as we could during the dinner rush. We were making sure the plates matched the ticket and making sure everything looked good before running it out to the table. Trevor noticed there was a missing piece of shrimp in one of the bowls, not knowing the other piece was hidden behind the mound of pasta. When he mentioned the shortage, he felt immediate backlash from the manager. The manager replied, "You don't think I can count? They just don't fuckin give you this position if you don't know how to count!" As he was saying this, flames from the grill were igniting over his shoulder, higher than him, as if the devil had been unleashed.

I immediately turned to Trevor and softly said, "Ignore him. You were just trying to help. You don't need to listen to that garbage." I expected the manager to hear what I said in order to prevent something like this from happening again. This trend happens way too often in the restaurant industry. F&B employees are mentally beaten down by their managers, and they do not stand a chance to fight back. They are already exhausted and emotionally spent. The industry becomes so systematic and routine that it feels like you have been on the Gravitron, struggling through the daily grind. It becomes methodical as if you are a programmed robot with a conscious hypnotically going through the motions. It takes the YOU out of YOU.

I had a new experience in the workforce when I joined the corporate world. I was employed in the financial services industry for approximately 4 years. I met a lot of great people during my tenure as an agent (Financial Services Professional). There were also a lot of untrustworthy agents and managers in the industry. The managers (or partners) had a team of agents, and expected to keep "activity" inside the team. Following the manager's example created a divide amongst members of the team. Not only was there a divide amongst team members, but it became a divide amongst agents within the team. Since it was a commission-based job, agents were constantly trying to generate leads. Agents often kept to themselves, and became protective of their leads when another agent inquired about their prospects, inevitably defeating any chance of forming a mastermind group. Agents may pair up once in a while, but for the most part, agents were on their own. The managers created a lot of competition amongst agents, which created friction in the office.

Many managers took a narcissistic approach, which became a trait many of the managers expected their agents to adopt. Their desire for control and lack of sympathy clearly showed they had a business to run, similar to a household led by a disciplinarian, maintaining control over you. Many are raised to respect people who climbed their way to the top, and it became customary to surrender. Initially, you accept it for what it is, or you quit. Most new agents dealt with a lot because they were led to believe they were unworthy of their position. This was an eye-opener for me as it was my first experience joining the corporate world after 10 great years of teaching. It reminded me of when I was a student with a strict teacher or principal multiplied by 10. I simply assumed this was how the corporate world operated, and the schools did everything they could to prepare us for the real world.

I did not like what appeared to be obsessive control in the office. I spent 3 of 4 years away from the office, mainly because of what seemed excessive given the situation. As much as you tried to ignore their personality traits, being around management caused you to inherit some of their traits. The ego is subtly formed through daily habits, and the narcissistic traits carry over into your personal life. Before you know it, you are miserable all the time. The only person that cheered me up was my beautiful wife, Amanda.

The negative environment led to drinking and eating like crap every other night at a local bar. As I carried this weight around, day in and day out, discussing commission checks so we could pay the bills, it was not fair to Amanda. As I continued falling down this downward spiral, I failed to see how detached I became from the world I loved. I became a cog in the system, stuck on the Gravitron, far from getting off. It took a major shift of awareness for me to wake up from the nightmare.

Staying in any one of these environments is not bad, as long as you are not staying in it for the long haul. You will feel yourself getting sucked in if you are in it for too long. You may make compromises with yourself, one after another, such as "I just need to make it through the summer," or "just through the holidays," or "the money's good." The longer you stay in the same environment, the more you will see your tolerance dwindle. You will become irritable about why you have to work when others do not. Before you know it, you will become numb to your situation, lose touch with reality, and accept your life for what it is. You should always carefully choose your work environment, with as much thought as purchasing a new home or buying a new car, especially if you plan on staying for the long haul. Your work environment is what you are feeding your mind 8 hours a day, 5 days a week. If you cannot separate your work life from your personal life, it will assimilate and transcend into who you become; there is no escaping until you leave.

Accumulate Experiences and Learn Perspectives

Do you remember how much the demographics changed when you made the leap from elementary to middle school? Middle school to high school? The demographics grew larger, and people invited their own uniqueness with them. What seemed different to you was unique to them. Students are bussed in from all over town to meet at one central point, causing everyone to adapt to their new environment. Instead of using this opportunity to learn about someone else's perspective and culture, we continue searching and attracting people we identify most with. Your view of reality is influenced by the environment you surround yourself with as what you perceive as normal.

Being in a new environment can be stressful and confusing, which is why it is common to seek people with similar qualities. By attracting like people, you will repeat the same habits you had in the first place, as the gravitational cycle continues to spin all around you; nothing changes except the people in your circle. Embrace diversity by stepping outside your comfort zone and meeting people that you have nothing in common with. You will get to learn what motivates and inspires them, what their background was like, what offends them, and learn from multiple perspectives rather than just one. The more diverse you are, the more you learn. You can plant a garden using one type of seed, but if you only have one crop, your garden will not be as exciting as if you planted 100 different types of seeds. Become a farmer of your environment and pick the right crops to fit your needs. Surround yourself with people that make you feel good and encourage growth. Embrace change and become accepting of all backgrounds. Every person you meet has a unique perspective. Welcome friendly, inviting, warm people in your life who are positive. Avoid people who are not willing to embrace change after attempting to learn from their perspective. The ones who are closed-minded, whose thoughts are dominated by negativity, are trapped in their own bubble and need to find their own way out. Maybe reading this book will awaken those who seek awareness. Always trust your intuition. If the friendship feels right or feels natural, then accept it for what it is. If you have a bad vibe around them, trust your instincts, and move on to someone who accepts you for who you are.

You will come across even greater diversity when working a job. No two jobs are similar, even if it is in the same industry. You will find one employer doing the same job differently than another in the same profession. Instead of judging which decision is better, understand the different techniques that are used by those who are knowledgeable in that field. Jobs are a dime a dozen. It is very easy to jump from one job to another. Gain as much experience and perspective as you can.

Stay in a workplace that inspires creativity, open-mindedness, and has a positive environment. When you first start, the working conditions are usually quite friendly. As you become settled in your new position, you might start to hear gossip from other employees. Gossip only leads to negativity in the workplace. Disengage with any destructive chatter. When this occurs, you will find the morale is low, so start thinking of an exit strategy. While you are planning your exit, learn as much as you can about the employer, the cause of the environment for its employees, and what you like and dislike about the system in place. Once you absorb all your resources by learning from different perspectives about how business is conducted, and have a sound exit strategy, then it is time to move on.

If you like your job and feel you are continuously growing and evolving, and it has a healthy working environment: keep going. Oftentimes, people make compromises within the job because it has "benefits." A person might feel they are advancing in their position from being a sales representative to a manager as they continue climbing the corporate ladder. This happens in almost all facets where advancement seems inevitable. In these cases, growth is an illusion. Ask yourself: do you really feel like you have advanced, or are you shifting positions within a system that encourages retention? If you come to the realization that you are only working in the system because of the benefits, you are less likely fulfilled with what you are doing. Do not work yourself to the point where you feel trapped in a system, delaying the inevitable. If that has become the case, quit. Humans are creatures of habit. Although it is easy to stay put, you will learn to adapt and find something different that actually encourages growth.

Keep your main focus on your true purpose. What are you truly passionate about? Is Monday your favorite day of the week? Pursue your passion with extreme focus and intent. The more experiences you accumulate from different environments, the more prepared you will be for the big picture in your life. At some point, everything you built will come together. Stay positive with all the people you meet, because you never know when your paths will line up again. The sentiment they have for you will be the exact same 5 years from now, regardless of how much you have changed. Do not allow yourself to become a prisoner of your past as you move on to the next chapter of your life. If you love what you do, you will not mind the journey.

How Do Others View You?

The image you have for yourself is completely different than how others view you. In retrospect, how you view others is not the same way they view themselves. Oftentimes, you allow yourself to become imprisoned with concern over how others view you. You created this image, or ego, which is how you expect people in your surroundings to view you. However, every person you come across, whether it be your parents, siblings, close friends, or people you go to school or work with, all view you in a different image. Deviating from your image will cause people in your environment to notice the sudden changes. Instead of dealing with ongoing confrontations about your apparent transition, you may revert to your old habits rather than dealing with conflicts, and continue to hide in the shell of your ego.

Your reputation will follow you around wherever you go, because you are repeating the same habits. You may find it more difficult to break free from your reputation the longer you remain in the same environment. Your self-perception reflects how others perceive you. You continue to attract those that fit your perception.

If you want to create a new image for yourself, become open-minded to change. Change your environment as often as possible and take in as many experiences as you can. Become the person you desire to be within your new environment. You will begin to notice a shift in how people view you. When you make the shift, notice how people treat you, and compare it to your previous experiences. When you notice positive movement, you will notice how much better you feel about yourself. You can always make changes and adapt along the way. Bounce from one experience to another, and discover new ways to enhance personal growth.

While you are improving your image, you will notice the various types of people you attract. People you normally would have not associated with are now entering your life. As you attract a higher quality of people, you will continue to evolve. When growth becomes stagnant, make the same leap again. It is up to you to become the better version of yourself. Do not worry how others view you. Who you attract is a reflection of yourself. You will see the person you are becoming by the people you are attracting into your life. You are progressing into a new person.

Create a YOU Image

The routine you create will lead to people having certain expectations of you. These expectations may feel like you are being controlled by your image. You may find yourself being viewed the same even if you are no longer the same person. Parents, siblings, teachers, classmates, and co-workers will treat you the same as you will find most people live in the past, not the present. Patterns repeat themselves based on how you and others think. As your thoughts become your reality and your future, repeating old thought habits will become your future. Replace old thought habits with new ones. It is very difficult to evolve and grow with someone when you are being reminded of your past.

As you change environments in an attempt to create a new image for yourself, you get to start with a clean slate. There are not any preconceived notions about you, so everything you create is fresh. Avoid toxic environments and behaviors you found in the past. Instead of eating out and having a few beers, watching TV, or staying out late at night, change up the routine and get some exercise, walk around the neighborhood, or join a yoga studio. Find activities that are engaging and that stimulate personal development. Associate with people who will help you become a better version of yourself. Align yourself with people who you share common goals and beliefs with. By changing environments, you can create a new belief system with people that will guide you towards who you want to become. Each person you grow with has the same intent as you. Two minds are more powerful than one. You are essentially growing together in accomplishing both of your desires, even when you do not have a common end-goal in mind. The team you create will become your mastermind group that will transform how you think.

After growing in your environment, you will eventually reconnect with people who remember you for who you were. They will quickly recognize your change in behavior. This may be uncomfortable for them, as they may think you are artificial or fake. They usually have a hard time distinguishing the difference between the old and new you, as they want you to change back to how they remember you. If you find yourself being pulled to a lower frequency and they do not accept you for who you have become, disengage with them. These people are stuck on the Gravitron and expect routine.

A shark can only grow 8 inches in a fish bowl but can grow over 8 feet when placed in an ocean. You cannot outgrow your environment unless you are willing to make a change. You have plenty of room for growth. YOU can choose to grow, no one else can do it for you. Surround yourself with people that tell you, "YOU CAN," and then, YOU WILL.

CHAPTER ELEVEN

POWER OF LOVE

Albert the Great

The most powerful force in the world is love. When you give love to things, your life will improve dramatically. Love is a force that cannot be seen or heard, it can only be felt. Love is the highest frequency. You do not have to see the strength of love to know it exists. Radio waves, microwaves, gravity, and Wi-Fi are all examples of things you cannot see, but know exist. Albert Einstein wrote a letter to his daughter regarding the nature of love, he wrote:

> "When I proposed the theory of relativity, very few understood me, and what I will reveal now to transmit to mankind will also collide with the misunderstanding and prejudice in the world.
>
> I ask you to guard the letters as long as necessary, years, decades, until society is advanced enough to accept what I will explain below.
>
> There is an extremely powerful force that, so far, science has not found a formal explanation to. It is a force that in-

cludes and governs all others, and is even behind any phenomenon operating in the universe and has not yet been identified by us. This universal force is LOVE.

When scientists looked for a unified theory of the universe, they forgot the most powerful unseen force. Love is Light, that enlightens those who give and receive it. Love is gravity, because it makes some people feel attracted to others. Love is power, because it multiplies the best we have, and allows humanity not to be extinguished in their blind selfishness. Love unfolds and reveals. For love we live and die. Love is God and God is Love.

This force explains everything and gives meaning to life. This is the variable that we have ignored for too long, maybe because we are afraid of love because it is the only energy in the universe that man has not learned to drive at will.

> " This universal force is LOVE. This force explains everything and gives meaning to life. "

To give visibility to love, I made a simple substitution in my most famous equation. If instead of $E = mc^2$, we accept that the energy to heal the world can be obtained through love multiplied by the speed of light squared, we arrive at the conclusion that love is the most powerful force there is, because it has no limits.

After the failure of humanity in the use and control of the other forces of the universe that have turned against us, it is urgent that we nourish ourselves with another kind of energy...

If we want our species to survive, if we are to find meaning in life, if we want to save the world and every sentient being that inhabits it, love is the one and only answer.

Perhaps we are not yet ready to make a bomb of love, a device powerful enough to entirely destroy the hate, selfishness and greed that devastate the planet.

However, each individual carries within them a small

but powerful generator of love whose energy is waiting to be released.

When we learn to give and receive this universal energy, dear Lieserl, we will have affirmed that love conquers all, is able to transcend everything and anything, because love is the quintessence of life.

I deeply regret not having been able to express what is in my heart, which has quietly beaten for you all my life. Maybe it's too late to apologize, but as time is relative, I need to tell you that I love you, and thanks to you I have reached the ultimate answer!"

Your father,
Albert Einstein

We have been taught to limit our love. We are expected to love our family and close friends. They are extensions of us and a reflection of ourselves, so it is important to express love in the way we would like to receive love. We are all connected even though two people are not alike. To better understand one another's adversity, place yourself in their shoes to understand their experiences.

You are conditioned to defend, limit, and protect love, and not use love so freely to reduce vulnerabilities from external forces. Love, peace, prosperity, unity, and togetherness are not taught regularly in today's curriculum. You are not taught how to use love or how to properly express it. Instead, you are taught throughout grade school that anger, aggression, power, control, hate, revenge, and deception are acceptable forms of behavior in society as a means to rebel against something that does not fit your vision. There is no good cause to destroy humanity and civilization for the sake of expansion for one's purpose. Instead of building up civilizations, the focus became the benefit of tearing them down. The events that led to where we are today expose a threat to humanity across the board, as it appears to be an accepted form of behavior.

We live in a competitive world. Individuals have a mindset that in order to get ahead in life, you need to be "better" than those around you, even if it leads to oppression. When people are viewed as a source of energy that can be bent, controlled, manipulated, and deceived in order to serve a higher entity's purpose, hostility will arise. People feel energy and vibrations. Oftentimes, they cannot put their finger on why they feel bitter and resentful, but the frequency is being felt all the time. Over time, negative emotions will ensue because integrity and love are constantly being dismissed.

Employers and bosses may create a workplace that limits growth potential because of the limited knowledge they are willing to share with you. They may feel that they have invested their money and time in you, so their immediate goal, aside from running a successful business, is retention. The business owner may 1) be afraid you will learn their business and become their competition, potentially stealing clients; 2) limit your growth potential because they fear you will leave; 3) feel they earned the right to become the boss so why should they share their secrets with you? This creates low morale within the company, especially if the work environment is already toxic. Employees may feel like a cog in a system that demonstrates repeat behaviors and performance.

A business can be successful without the need for power and control. The employer should create a workspace that encourages growth and potential. It does not matter how big or small the company is, create a work environment the employee will love going to so they will not want to leave. Employers should listen to their employees as if they are family. Demonstrate compassion and love, and treat each employee individually. If not for each employee, the business would fail. Offer profit sharing as an incentive. The goal for the employer is to allow their loyal employees to continue to grow and expand in the company, teach them every aspect about the business with the possibility of being able to leave, but create a work environment that the employee will not want to leave. If the employee concludes that running a business is a lot more work than they have been led to believe, the employee may be comfortable staying in an hourly/salary role rather than taking on the task of starting their own business. This will develop mutual respect between the employer and employee.

Love is the greatest form of power. Whether you own a business or are an employee, lead by example and show compassion for your colleagues, employees, and customers. You will create an environment that will be hard to leave, missed when you are gone, and keep customers coming back. The world is already hard enough. Express love.

Love Brings US Together

Love should not be limited to just the people in your life. It should be expressed to everyone around as well. Have empathy for those who are not expressing love, as they do not have it to share yet. You cannot give something you do not have. Those who lack love do not love themselves. Fill them with love and love will find them.

We should be looking at ways to improve the lives of those in less developed nations without the concern of profit. We live in a world of abundance and should extend the cause for all of humanity. Every person across the globe is equally valuable, and should be treated as such. When we can all show love for one another, the world will experience a power that has never been felt. Imagine if we connected the world with love all around us, harnessing the power of love globally, rather than war, greed, takeover, or fear-based tactics as a form of control. When we begin to use love as the only tactic of human evolution, humanity across the board will thrive.

Love What You Have

Love should not be limited to people. Love should be expressed towards what you have. When I was changing schools (three schools in five years), then driving all over the state in the four years of working in the financial services industry, before returning back to the classroom as a substitute teacher and while discovering my passion, one thing remained constant – my car! I was a teacher in the Charleston area for five years before moving to a financial firm. Upon joining the financial firm, the manager encouraged new agents to upgrade their vehicle, because it would give clients the illusion that they were successful, so they would be more likely to buy from them. He recommended the Mercedes C-class. I was not much of a car guru, but I felt the need to upgrade my vehicle in order to have the feeling of success.

I drove my car all over the place. I drove it to Michigan numerous times for the holidays along with driving all over the state of South Carolina, mostly for work. I could not afford the Mercedes at the time, and did not appreciate my car. I felt the constant need for an "upgrade" to show my true worth. I resented the fact that I still owned a 2008 Saturn Vue, when I felt like I worked hard enough that I should be able to upgrade to a reasonably priced luxury vehicle. It always felt like I was one or two nice cases away from being able to purchase one of my favorite types of vehicles, an Audi. I did not have a specific type of Audi, but just knew it represented a status symbol of "success." I felt I would be happy if I traded in the Saturn Vue for the Audi.

After leaving the financial services industry, I still desired a vehicle upgrade. During this time, I began a journey of showing gratitude for things that I had, but I still did not appreciate my vehicle. It was 10 years old and I felt ready for a new one. I felt like an upgrade was inevitable and only a matter of time. The universe continued to send me messages to wait on purchasing a new vehicle. Then one day, in the summer of 2019, I had a flashback of all the journeys I had with my car. Upon reflection, it dawned on me that my car had been there whenever I needed it and had never let me down. Aside from minor fixes from wear and tear, it had been dependable. Then suddenly, I had this sense of gratitude for my car. If not for my car, I would not be in the position I am in today. My car has been extremely reliable for over 200,000 miles and counting. I love my car and plan on driving it for the next 200,000 miles. This car is a part of me.

You become a part of everything you come into contact with. What you put out in the universe, you shall receive. When you do not appreciate the things that you have, you are telling the universe you do not deserve them. This is a mentality of having lack, and when you do not appreciate what you own, you will receive less. When you appreciate everything: the car you drive, the house or apartment you live in, the clothes you wear, the shoes you own, the food you eat, they all carry a frequency and become a part of you. When you give love and gratitude for the things you are in contact with, you are speaking the universal language and will attract more abundance into your life.

When I was out searching for a new car, it never felt right. I felt like I was abandoning a paid-up car in order to add a new car payment into my life. My intuition kept telling me to not purchase a new vehicle because I did not need it. My ego was telling me to purchase a new car to symbolize my social status for people I had never met. With my understanding that ego is a self-created illusion, I became more aware of who I was. I now have a new sense of gratitude for my car, and love my car. After having negative thoughts about my car and wanting it to be replaced, I now want this car to be in my life for years and years to come.

Love Yourself First!

The first person you need to love is yourself. If you do not love yourself, you cannot expect other people to love you. Other people cannot fill the void of love for you. Once you love yourself, you will become a human magnet and begin to attract love. You are attracting what you are, not what you want. You will attract love from all other entities around you by giving off love. Love the material things you currently possess. Show gratitude and love for everything you have, because there are millions, if not billions of people in this world who would trade positions with you overnight. Instead of feeling like you are owed more, or that you deserve more in life, be grateful for what you have and love everything that comes into your life.

Do not sit around and complain all day, especially about events that are beyond your control. Once an event happens, it has happened. Spending more time on it only takes away from focusing your energy on positive things. People who complain about everything, whether it is an event, something they watched on TV, the news, or a certain obstacle they are dealing with, such as high blood pressure, the stock market going down, a pinched nerve, a cracked windshield, or spilling their coffee, will continue to attract similar events in their life. When you choose to focus on negativity, you attract more negativity. Everything you see, hear and how you react is a reflection of yourself. You are actually complaining about yourself when you complain about the things around you. Choose to love yourself first, and you will find there is less to complain about.

When the Last Thing Is Love

Over the holidays, I overheard my sister bring up an issue she had with her phone service carrier. She mentioned that even though she returned the items, she was still being charged $60 for something that was already paid. I faced a similar situation with two other phone companies. One was for $450 and the other was for $80. She and I had a receipt and kept disputing the charge. We did not want to pay the amount out of principle. Instead of paying the amount after submitting receipts and filing a claim, the companies sent the amount owed to collections. My credit score took a significant hit as a result. Therefore, I was willing to trade my time and credit score for the principle of the matter. It was a waste of energy which could have been redirected into something more positive. The good news behind this is that even though at the time I did not understand why I was being penalized for something I did not deserve, I was able to share my insight with my sister so she could avoid a similar situation.

People attract debt because of how they think. The cycle continues to repeat itself because of their mindset. Most people do not see a connection between winning the lottery and becoming broke again, or earning a holiday bonus only to have it wither away due to an unforeseen debt obligation. For example, I was working a side gig over the holidays and the hiring manager mentioned that they did not have a savings account. They were planning on using their holiday bonus to begin a new savings account. Upon receiving the holiday bonus, they were not grateful for what they received and discussed their displeasure with the employees, mocking what a small amount it was. Feeling ungrateful leads the universe to responding accordingly.

Within a week of receiving the holiday bonus, they were driving to work, hit a pothole, and blew out their tire on a two-lane road, making it impossible to turn on the shoulder of the road. They had to drive another mile before turning off into a nearby parking lot. They suffered rim damage and had to have the tire and rim completely replaced. The cost was $230, evaporating their holiday bonus.

However, people continue to attract these cycles when they expect them to happen. When you express love and gratitude, you are raising your frequency. When your frequency becomes elevated, you will encounter fewer negatives. In all likelihood, if they loved their bonus, and expressed gratitude for the amount, chances are the unforeseen event and expense would not have happened. You are lowering your frequency when you express greed and displeasure versus raising your frequency with love and gratitude. When you speak out into the universe, be careful what you say. Negative energy will always attract negative energy. A person who encounters unforeseen debt attracts it because their negative energy was put out in the universe.

Sincere about Love

Every holiday season, I debate whether or not I should drive or fly back to Michigan. Some years I could not make it due to the weather conditions. Flying was not always a financial option for me as well. After missing the previous year due to bad weather, I was faced with a dilemma of whether to drive or fly. I was leaning towards driving back until the universe answered my question. I was substitute teaching at the School of the Arts on Monday, December 9, 2019. According to the sub plans, I had to take my group of students to the Black Box and watch the Christmas play, performed by the junior class. This was exciting. Free live entertainment by future Hollywood performers.

These students did an amazing job. Such a great performance by the talented actors and actresses on stage. They performed a wonderful, feel-good story, which an audience of all ages could relate to. This performance was as good as Broadway. The director did an outstanding job preparing the cast, and the cast was very talented and professional. The portrayal of their characters gave their audience a sense of emotion anyone can relate to – LOVE.

This play triggered the emotions of love, unity, togetherness, faith, hope, happiness, and manifesting desires into reality. The actors and actresses harnessed their emotions regarding love with one ultimate power – SINCERITY. The secret is to be sincere in everything you do. Every character you play (ego or on stage), role at work, focusing on your purpose with intention, all must have sincerity behind the mask. When you are sincere with passion and love, and use sincerity with determination and focus on what you need to do, you will be able to manifest your desires when you are sincere about love. The cast was doing a great job at demonstrating that.

While enjoying the play, I made the decision that I must do whatever I could to make it home for the holiday season. Since it was Monday, I decided to wait until Tuesday to look for a flight since the cost is rumored to be cheaper on Tuesday versus any other day of the week. After the play, I said to myself, "I hope I get to sub for these kids tomorrow. I really want to thank them for their performance." (Side note – when you are a substitute teacher, you already know what school and teacher you are subbing for the next day, but you do not necessarily know what kids.)

The following day, I just so happened to be subbing for that same exact junior class who performed the play. It was a US History class, one of the subjects I taught when I was a full-time teacher. After thanking and congratulating them on their performance, I shared that it was something I needed to see to help me get through a hurdle. Their faces lit up like a Christmas tree, like it was something they needed to hear as well. When we put time and energy into something, it feels good to be noticed for it. Whenever you are in a position to make someone feel better about themselves, like the junior class did for me, let them know immediately. Do not wait till tomorrow. I thanked them again before being dismissed from class. When you are expressing gratitude, you are expressing love. Love is the power of giving. You are giving consent to those you support for their calling. Gratitude confirms their beliefs and offers validation that they are on the right track. In turn, they will feel the power of love from the gratitude you expressed, raising their frequency and vibration. Love can be spread contagiously like a virus, and has the power to save humanity across the globe.

The students helped me decide to purchase a plane ticket versus driving back. Their performance also helped me remember that the most important things in your life are the people you surround yourself with. There is no greater gift than the people you surround yourself with. The greatest gift you can give and receive is the gift of love. Everything else is meaningless. The meaning you put into something is arbitrary from person to person, but the meaning you put in love with your family, friends, and the people you come into contact with is more powerful and beautiful than anything else.

Babies Are Love

You have been programmed on how to think since birth. When a baby is born, it does not have any form of beliefs. The beliefs are taught to a baby, and it continues to be conditioned until it learns how to think. Their belief system becomes planted so deep in their subconscious mind that it becomes hardwired into their habits. A person's habits are actions without thought.

Humans have these expectations that they must raise their children similar to how they were raised, or even better than what they had. A new parent may have ideas of what they can do to improve their child's life from the beginning, by teaching them family values, morals, etc., similar to how they were raised. During a child's upbringing, they are taught their limitations and constantly compared to the development of other children around the same age. They are often praised for their achievements and scolded for what they lack. They become afraid to take risks and fall into the conventional norms of society. Inevitably, the child creates their own limitations based on the belief system that was implanted in them, encompassed by fear. Fear of failure. Fear of expression. Fear of rejection. Fear of loss.

People develop these fears over time. These fears are usually taught, and not from personal experience or observation. Fear is a false belief system, which is developed from birth. The baby is born with two fears: fear of falling and fear of loud noises. The rest of their fears are taught to them. The parent feels like they should control their child with what they say, but a parent's actions are instilled in a child as learned behavior. If the child is out in the yard playing with a lizard, and the parent comes out and screams, "Ahhhh, there's a lizard," the child will suddenly be afraid of lizards.

There would be a greater chance for humanity to survive if we made one small change – parents must learn from their children, beginning from birth. Babies are born with the most amount of love to give. The most valuable expression they want to show is love. Instead of having to teach a child what you know, the child teaches you what you do not know. Children are born scientists and are creatures of habit. They will discover what they can and cannot do without being told. Of course, there are limitations. The child should be taught the consequences of fire, gravity, chemicals, jumping into a pool, and other safety issues. However, overall, the child has the power to bring unity to the family with their expression of love.

I personally believe babies are spirit guides transformed into human form. Since the majority of us are unaware of spirit guides, let alone how to communicate with them, the spirit guides use methods to try and connect the spiritual world to the physical world. It is up to you to see the messages. The spirit guides are transmuted from the spiritual dimension into the physical world through the medium of a person. The spirit enters into the baby upon birth to send a message to help save and heal a hurting family, and to encourage love, happiness, and unity. You immediately notice a family coming together once a child is born.

The majority of us are looking for a higher meaning in life, questioning life's purpose. Most of us are lost because we become imprisoned by these false belief systems that have been created for us. They control how we think, teach us that war and aggression are more valuable than love and expression, and we fail to recognize the messages the universe is sending on an ongoing basis. We can learn how to benefit from the messages the universe is sending, instead of reacting negatively or ignoring them altogether when they do not match a belief system. When everyone begins to follow messages from the universe, they will see that love is the first form of expression being sent. As soon as we can harness this energy, and use the power of love as the first form of expression, we will begin a new wave this planet has not seen.

Summary

As previously stated, people are energy. Whether the energy is positive or negative, the universe will respond according to the energy and frequency you are sending out. When you are sending love out into the universe, you are sending out the highest form of positive energy; therefore, you will receive the highest form of energy in return. You cannot control what happens in your life, but you can control how you respond. Do not allow yourself to be controlled by negative energy because negative events will continue to follow you around. When you surround yourself with negative people, you will continue to attract negative people. If the negative person is a family member or loved one, lead by example with positive energy. No one has the power to control your mind and energy. When you give someone permission to control your ability to think, you lose your control of your mind.

Love works for everything you connect with in life, including material things. Instead of being greedy and feeling owed or acting as though you deserve more abundance in your life, be grateful for what you already have. By giving love to material things, you are in actuality giving love to yourself for the choices you made when purchasing these items. It was important to you when you bought the item, and it brought you value while owning it. By sending more love out into the universe, you will attract more love.

Chapter Twelve

ATTITUDE IS EVERYTHING

Choose Your 'Tude!

People either choose to be happy, or they choose to be miserable. Happy people embrace whatever situation life throws at them. Miserable people may feel sorry for themselves when faced with adversity or find a problem with every solution. When someone says, "They made me angry." What they are really saying is that they allowed someone else to control their emotions. You cannot control everything that happens to you, but you have complete control over how you respond. Once an event occurs, the next step in the process is to choose how you wish to react. Choosing the right attitude is the difference between being happy or miserable.

Whenever I was feeling miserable and had a bad attitude about something, my adorable wife, Amanda, would say to me, "Change your 'tude, turd! Change. Your. 'Tude." Or when I came home from a long exhausting day of work and complained to her, Amanda cheerfully was quick to say "It's otayyy." She was right! It was okay. There was nothing in this world that bothered me the second I was in front of her. Everything that I felt the need to complain about no longer existed when she was in my presence. All that mattered was being with her, nothing else. You have the ability to choose what makes you happy and what makes you miserable. The good news is you are in control of your 'tude!

Regardless of financial status, every person has dealt with obstacles and adversity in their lives. Most people who are not millionaires think millionaires have it easy because they do not have bills to pay or debt to worry about. It is all about perspective. Jim Carrey said, "I think everybody should get rich and famous and do everything they ever dreamed of, so they can see that it's not the answer." The answer is in your attitude.

You cannot speak for someone else without walking in their shoes. It is impossible to know what challenges and hardships another person is dealing with. People develop habits in their subconscious mind at a very young age, which then become hardwired in their brain. The way someone behaves towards you is a reflection of their attitude, not yours. Do not allow their negative attitude to control the way you think. The way you respond and react is developed in your habits from a very young age, ingrained in your subconscious mind, giving the illusion you do not have a choice in your actions.

A person's actions are only a reflection of how they wish to engage. Any event can trigger a response, developed from their subconscious mind. Their actions can be from their upbringing, what they have seen as an "acceptable form of behavior" on TV or in their household, and who they associate with as it resembles their environment. When a person becomes loud, belligerent, or argumentative, they may come from an environment where their parents are strict disciplinarians, controlling their actions. Since they are not given the freedom to make choices at home, with their voices suppressed by parents and older siblings under the hierarchy of control, they may act out while out in public.

A person's upbringing can impact how they are perceived. They will likely have good intentions behind their actions because they saw it as an accepted form of behavior. When you recognize it as such, you begin to attract like beings in your reality, which simply extends the form of acceptance. Upon discovering that how you were conditioned to think is different from your peers, you might begin to feel resentful towards those who taught you to think a certain way. What you thought was an acceptable form of behavior is now considered wrong, and you are just learning about this now. Who is to blame? You may find yourself placing blame on others for your shortcomings, instead of accepting responsibility.

Choosing the right attitude can be the difference between being broke or being a millionaire. It is also the difference between being happy or miserable. You are constantly communicating with the universe. Whether you are communicating internally or externally, your messages are being heard. How you respond to something can have a tremendous impact on your life. The way you respond today will snowball into how you respond tomorrow.

Having a positive attitude can have a significant impact on what happens in your daily life. If you are met with misfortune, instead of being negative about it, ask yourself what can be learned from this experience. How will this experience today help you become a better person tomorrow? If you choose to be negative and play the victim, no one will feel sorry for you. People are dealing with their own battles, and some may enjoy hearing of your setbacks. After all, misery loves company. As bad as you think you have it, there are a lot more people out there who have it worse than you. Again, it is all about perspective.

You may engage with a lot of people during your daily life. Some people are always happy, and other people are always miserable, and others are neutral – happy one day and miserable the next. The super happy person might be dealing with a lot more struggles at home and in their personal life than you have ever imagined. The happy person is choosing to be happy, while the miserable person is choosing to be miserable. As Wayne Dyer states,

> " Everything is either an opportunity to grow, or an obstacle to keep you from growing. "

"With everything that has happened to you, you can either feel sorry for yourself, or treat what has happened as a gift. Everything is either an opportunity to grow, or an obstacle to keep you from growing. You get to choose."

We are put on this earth

for a reason. You will find your purpose in life when you choose to have a positive attitude. You will start to see immediate results when you begin to choose a positive attitude. You will attract more positivity when you respond positively. Even when something bad happens, analyze the situation to determine what can be gained from the experience. When your dominating thoughts are positive, you will have a positive experience. Develop a habit of being positive with everything that has happened in your life by taking it one day at a time. Show gratitude for what the universe sends you, and the universe will continue sending you more positive encounters.

Look at each experience, whether good or bad, from a broader perspective. Imagine playing chess, and the chess pieces move based on the attitude each piece has. Reflect on each chess piece move and understand why the move took place. If it was a move in the positive direction, analyze why it became a favorable move and what can be learned from it. When a chess piece moves against you, instead of dwelling on the negative move, reflect on why the move happened and how it can be avoided in the future. Do not let the highs get too high or the lows get too low. Embrace each move as if the universe is moving in synchronicity with you, not against you. Attract when something responds favorably, repel when something happens negatively. Attract what you want, not what you don't want.

Positive 'Tude Leads to Positive Results

Your reality is the result of what you say and think over a long period of time. How you respond to every event is a reflection of your attitude. When you are on an ascending frequency, you will eventually achieve the result you are seeking. However, the goal you are expecting to achieve will never happen in an upward linear fashion like you hope it will. If something bad happens, it does not mean you have fallen off your trajectory. It simply means the negative event created a void in order to clear the way for something positive to fill the gap. Imagine your body is equivalent to running on a full cup of water. If the cup is full, you are unable to make way for more water to be added to the cup. In order to add new water to the cup, you must remove some of the old water. The universe takes away something to help place you back on the path you are seeking. These negative events are usually the trigger you need to reestablish focus.

When you were a young child, your natural instincts protected you. You knew when something did not feel right and you trusted your intuition. Your intuitive nature is your sixth sense. Trust your sixth sense by listening to your feelings and instincts. When something goes wrong, take a step back and observe the situation instead of feeling like the victim. When you continue playing the victim, you will attract more negative things in your life. Take a step back and reflect on why something bad happened and choose to have a positive attitude from the experience. When you do this, you can change the pattern of your day from negative to positive.

If you start your morning by spilling coffee on your pants, burning your neck with the curling iron, or pulling your breakfast out of the fridge, accidentally spilling blueberries all over the floor, do not dwell on what happened. Slow down and reflect on why this happened. When negative events take place, you are out of sync with the universe. You can fix this by changing the way you think. Think of the positives that came from each event. If you spilled coffee on your pants, think to yourself at least you are at home and you can switch into a new pair of pants. If you burn yourself with a curling iron, say to yourself at least it is not going to scar and the hair will cover the burn mark; even if it did scar, you will have a story to tell. If you drop your container of blueberries all over the floor (like I did this morning), say to yourself, at least it was not a glass container, and the blueberries that hit the floor can still be rinsed off.

Another thought that crossed my mind after spilling the blueberries was that at least it was not a sauce or a liquid which would have been a lot messier to clean. When I had that thought, I noticed a container of marinara sauce that had been sitting in the fridge for over a week. It could easily have spilled. Chances are I will not be using it anytime soon, so I promptly threw it away. I took the sign from the universe after the blueberries spilled and threw away the container of marinara sauce because it could have been the next to spill. The important thing is to have the right attitude when something bad happens.

Not with that Attitude

You often overhear negative self-talk from others. Things like, "I can't get good grades," "I won't make the team," "I'm not smart enough," "I can't afford that," or "I won't ever be wealthy." My response to them is, "Not with that attitude." Your thoughts become things, your desires are manifested through faith, and your reality responds to your attitude which impacts your frequency.

The more you visualize something bad happening, the more likely you will attract it. Too many people have this "I told you so" mentality and need to be right 100% of the time, even when facts are in front of them. When they have to be right, their attitude is always negative, which leads to anger and resentment. When they continue to reaffirm a negative, at some point it will manifest into their reality because they have already visualized it and felt it as their reality. Even when you attempt to offset a negative by sayings things like "I don't want my car to break down" or "No more setbacks so we can start making money," you are reaffirming the outcome by putting your negative thoughts out in the universe, which will inevitably manifest into your reality.

Identify the types of personalities you surround yourself with. Whether it is from a parent, employer or boss, colleague or friend, remove yourself from your ego and look at the big picture of who you associate with. Does the person generally have a positive or negative attitude? Are they controlling, micromanaging, and critical of your decisions? Do they embrace your thoughts or discourage you from your growth potential? Again, you can never please a narcissist. A narcissist will continue to want more from you, which can be mentally and emotionally draining as you continue to second-guess yourself, feeling weak in the process. When you are in a toxic relationship with a narcissist, one thing is certain, they will never be happy with the results. The results become expectations, and the setbacks are viewed as failures.

When these people enter your life, do your best to avoid them. If they cannot be avoided, do not let their words impact how you feel. It will only impact you if you let it. Their attitude is a reflection of *themselves*, not you. Do not get sucked into their world, or you may live in constant misfortune and setbacks. Instead of trying to change someone, let them continue to be the person they are, and you continue being the person you aspire to be.

Train your mind to see the good in every situation. When you put your imagination to good use for a positive desired outcome, the same principle applies. Visualize what you want to receive, and use your five physical senses to create the feeling that it already exists. When you do this, and it becomes your passion, the feeling of existence will affirm itself. The universe will sync up to your beliefs and you will get what you desire. But it all starts with your attitude!

Keep your attitude positive, and positive things will unfold. Trust the process. Enjoy the journey and raise your awareness onto a higher frequency as often as possible. You get to choose your attitude, whether it is positive or negative. It is not about what happens to you, it is how you respond.

When you put your imagination to use, your thoughts will manifest into your desired outcomes, which will be a reflection of your attitude. You have to visualize what you want, see it as if it was already in your possession, and have the feeling as if it already exists. Replace "I can't" with "I can" by changing your perspective. Be accountable for your actions and the results will follow.

Universe Redirects

Getting fired from a job can be one of the worst feelings you can have. It will be even more devastating if you have a bad attitude as a result. You may think of all the negatives that come with the loss of income until it becomes the only thing you can think about. One thing that should be taken into consideration is what can be gained from the loss.

I learned that I could list my primary residence as a short-term rental on a popular website as a source of income. It felt like a business opportunity that would enable me to put my creativity to the test, and became a plan I wished to expand upon. In addition to my primary residence, I listed my timeshare. I acquired another property near my residence with a couple investors I went to college with back in Michigan. Short-term rentals became my new passion, and I loved the idea of sharing my experience with acquaintances who were new to the idea. What I mostly loved about the business was that I could put my creative touches to work, and keep expanding on my ideas.

However, the city had other plans. After a year, the city implemented a new policy that required rental properties to become compliant with the city. Since the application to relist was about a two-month process, I was forced to delist my primary residence. I did not have another source of income to support me. The loss of income forced me to seek employment elsewhere. Up until this point, I had spent my extra time, from April-September, renovating and running the investment property on my own. Since the income from the investment property was deferred, I did not expect to receive any financial support from the property anytime soon. Instead of being upset about the delisting, I used it as motivation to find a job.

Prior to delisting my property, I kept thinking that I felt stagnant with the short-term rental business. I no longer felt like I was growing, and it seemed like I was back on the Gravitron once again, performing the same routine tasks. I either needed to acquire a few more properties or do something totally different. The universe responded accordingly, by taking away something in order to gain something more significant in return. I found myself back in the classroom as a substitute teacher, a position I truly loved prior to being a full-time teacher.

I was excited to get back in the classroom once again. This position brought far more value to the lives of many, something I would have not realized had I not been required to delist. This new position provided me with an additional source of income, something I was able to cling onto once I was able to relist my property. However, the new income stream was secondary compared to the value I was getting from being back in the classroom. Being in the classroom felt like home to me, and became the spark I was seeking to put me back on a path towards my purpose.

Having the right attitude when faced with adversity put me in line with my calling. Instead of feeling sorry for myself and fighting the system, I chose to embrace the change of pace and reflected on how I could use it to my advantage. I was not a victim when I was forced to delist. The universe matched itself with my frequency in order to align with my purpose. A different outcome may have presented itself if I'd had a negative attitude.

Having a negative attitude can be detrimental to your growth. Imagine being an assistant coach of a high school football team. You have been coaching for seven years, and love everything about the position. The kids love you, and year after year, you identify with success as a winning coach. You won a few league championships, and gained respect from players and coaches around the league. You are associated with winning.

The following season, the head coach moves away, and the new coach wants to bring in their own assistant coaches to the program. Your services are no longer required, as the new coach wants to bring in his own culture. Instead of taking this as an opportunity to seek a head coaching position elsewhere, or move up to the college level, you let the news devastate you. You feel miserable about what transpired and decide to give up coaching altogether.

By choosing a negative attitude, you are losing out on an opportunity to grow in your position. Sitting back and feeling sorry for yourself will not benefit you in any situation. When faced with adversity, raise your frequency. The universe is not punishing you. It is clearing space for you by opening a door that was previously closed due to being complacent in your previous position. The universe is always communicating with you. Listen to what it is saying, choose the right attitude, and expect to receive.

With every failure comes a new opportunity to learn and develop. Failure is a mindset. It does not exist when you are persistent. Each failure is a pivot point. When you pivot, and learn from your experience, you will continue to evolve and grow. You will never find your purpose and comfort when you dwell on the past. If you focus on the past, you will be stuck on the past and will not be able to move forward.

We are humans, and humans are prone to making mistakes. Owning up to your mistakes is the first step. You should never feel remorse when you are being humanized. It is a part of life. Never place blame on your misfortunes, and more importantly, do not let a series of events doom you into finding your purpose. You are not a hostage of your past. Forgive yourself when you make a mistake because you may not have known how bad the mistake was until you experienced how bad the event made you feel. Not repeating the same mistake shows you are evolving through trial and error. How you respond to adversity will be the difference between finding your true calling or living with regret.

When you have consistent habits, whether it be positive or negative, and do the same thing over and over again, your life becomes too routine. You will not experience many highs or lows, as you develop this sense of complacency. Your habits become your foundation. In order to experience growth, you need to step outside your comfort zone. The universe will send you messages in order to shake you off your routine and redirect you into your true calling. If you look at the shakeup as an obstacle that you are unable to overcome, it becomes your fate. When you look at it as a pivot point to grow from, you will excel.

CHAPTER THIRTEEN

MAKE MONDAY YOUR FAVORITE DAY OF THE WEEK

While I was substitute teaching, a student asked, "How do you know when you've found your purpose?" I replied, "When Monday becomes your favorite day of the week." If you love Mondays, then likely you are on the right path. The majority of people dread Mondays, and live for the weekends. We have been made to believe that dreading Monday is a part of life, something we should all get used to. We celebrate Friday, weekends, and holidays as if we could enjoy them forever, only to return to the dreadful job we are putting up with for the next 30+ years of our lives.

You should not tolerate anything you are not enjoying, especially a job. If Monday is not your favorite day of the week, it is time to rethink your situation. Do not sacrifice your time, energy, and purpose in exchange for money when it becomes a disruption to your purpose. Money does not buy happiness. It buys you things, and will lead to buying more things as you become materialistic to feel validated, and fill the void of your desires. When you take a job, find something that will either lead to your purpose, or not be a distraction from your purpose. We all need money to survive. A nice-paying job by a healthy, positive company may provide you with the social aspect you are looking to achieve, or simply be a detour from your purpose. Jobs are not roadblocks unless you allow them to be. 98% of the population does not find their purpose, and becomes complacent about what life hands them.

Imitation leads to fixed habits. We are surrounded by people who develop our fixed habits through instruction and observation. We may find that we have not developed the skill to think for ourselves, because we fell into a cycle of repeated patterned behaviors: we have been taught to follow. It is the reason that when we graduate high school and college, we do not have a definitive aim in life. While being a follower, we develop conditioned habits. Habits become routine, which later becomes a fixed lifestyle. Set your intentions about what you expect to gain from life, and put a plan together to see it through.

Job Expectations

After we graduate high school or college, our goal is to find a job within our field. A lot of times you are inadvertently misdirected by your parents, teachers, and friends, only because they think they know what is best for you. Your mentors may attempt to direct you into a field they think you will be good at and enjoy because they would enjoy it if they were in your position. As you start listening to them, you become hopeful that your excitement will match theirs. During this time, you are unaware that they are the ones pulling the strings, while you are the one doing all the work.

A job does not bring you value if you are just showing up, going through the motions, and collecting a paycheck. Most people take the first job that is offered after graduation because it is expected, even though it is not the right job for them. You may also take this job because you either believe something better will not come along or you can find something better down the line. As you become glamorized by the pay increase from your previous position, the new job merely becomes something you can temporarily tolerate, distracting you from your ultimate purpose. Before you know it, years have passed by as you no longer find the job enjoyable. Your job becomes part of your routine and you rationalize the value of the amount of time you have invested. Keeping the same dissatisfied job is like throwing good money after bad, regardless of your degree. Your future is your "good money," and your miserable situation is your "bad money." You do not want to keep placing your future YOU in a position that will prolong your misery.

Having a job is not a bad thing. A job can be used as a building block towards your purpose. If you need a job for financial gain, you have not lost sight of your true purpose. As long as you keep your focus on your main purpose, a job might simply be a detour. However, if you find yourself trapped in the same job, ultimately pulling you from your purpose, it is time to develop a backup plan so that you can leave. You need to set high expectations for yourself and create a list of goals to stay on your path. Your goals should be a clear guide of what you expect to achieve from your source of income, as it leads to your true purpose.

New Jobs = New Experiences

Take on all kinds of jobs for research purposes, personal growth, and to gain more experience. By taking on different types of employment, you learn how different businesses operate. You will be able to identify what works, what does not work, what types of employees to hire or stay away from as you prepare to build your brand, and learn from multiple perspectives. You will notice each employer/company takes on a life of their own.

Each business has a system of operations in order to remain consistent with their agenda. We are expected to conform to the plan set in place, not create a new system, even if a new system would be more effective or efficient. Determine a few things about the company as you gain a broader perspective. Where is the pulse of the company? The heartbeat? What are the moving pieces? Once you feel like you have absorbed all your resources and are no longer growing, it's time to move on. With the experience, you will develop a broad form of intelligence as to how a company operates, which can be applied to growth in your personal position, whether it be in your own company, or seeking a position at a higher level.

Journey After Graduating

After earning a degree in communications, I had no idea what I wanted to do for the rest of my life. Most jobs I was interested in required 3-5 years of experience. I continued as a substitute teacher, since I loved being in the classroom. I was given the impression by my peers, colleagues, and societal norms that time was ticking away. With that in mind, I had this feeling of urgency to put my degree to good use, or attend graduate school. Since I really enjoyed substitute teaching, I went back to school and earned a teaching degree.

The decision was not made on my own. I kept hearing my dad and colleagues saying that I should be a teacher. I liked the idea of improving the lives of our youth, along with higher pay, stability of income, benefits, and being in a controlled environment. I never felt comfortable with routine, and being restricted on what I could teach did not feel right. I felt I would be basically putting myself in a bubble, inevitably turning into a shell of myself. I simply assumed having *any* profession would have restrictions, as the transition into adulthood meant building my career.

I now had a defined plan in place after graduating with a post baccalaureate degree in education. It was another check off the grocery list of achievements in order to be considered "successful." The next step on the agenda was to find a teaching job. I am not a fan of cold weather to say the least, and despised the idea of being stuck in Michigan for the next 30 years. Amanda and I decided to embark on a journey and move closer to the beaches in South Carolina. Upon moving, Amanda was hired as a dental assistant, and I was hired as a 7th grade history teacher; we were extremely excited about this new opportunity. Everything seemed to be going to plan, according to our belief system. We had taken our first steps into "adulting."

As the year progressed, I became miserable with my current situation. The commute was nearly an hour away, the students were disrespectful, and the administrators were not supportive of the teachers. We had a hard time finding substitute teachers for our classroom, so we were discouraged from missing any days unless we "had to." I did not understand the concept of a mental health day as a new teacher, so I took on the daily grind and missed school as little as possible.

The days began to feel longer, and I started to feel trapped in my situation, and anxiety kicked in. Fortunately, it was hard to stay miserable, because I had the utmost support at home. Every time I walked in the door and saw Amanda's beautiful smile, I reminded myself how lucky I was, and that I was doing the right thing. I reassured myself that this school and classroom were temporary and would only get better. I just figured it was first year jitters and all the wrinkles would naturally iron themselves out on their own.

As predicted, the following year changed as I was hired to teach high school. The assignment was at the alternative school in the district. These were students who either chose to be at this school because of its much smaller environment, or students who were sent there after being expelled. I chose this position because I felt like I could make an impact on these kids, and prepare them for society.

Unfortunately, I became discouraged within the first year when I did not feel I was making the impact I thought I should. There was a lot of negativity and anger in the classroom that was passed along and spread to the teachers. As much as I tried to disassociate myself, faculty members would play some colorful pranks that involved the students, which I was not too fond of. The pranks were playful at times, such as placing my stapler in a container filled with Jell-O, or having my car wrapped in newspaper with a bow on top prior to the holiday break, but the sentiment amongst the teacher in particular, and her students was more revengeful than spirited.

The negative energy and poor attitudes throughout the school were draining. I was having anxiety on a regular basis, and the teaching job felt like it was more about being controlled by the environment than being in control of myself. I felt like I was being pulled by the wrist, in a direction I did not want to travel, mentally, physically, and spiritually, like I was sucked onto the Gravitron.

I kept making excuses for myself and my situation, saying I was only teaching in my minor (history) and that my situation would be much better once I found a performing arts position. Also, the school hours and commute were ridiculous. I had to be on the road at 5:15 a.m. every morning in order to make it to school by 6:15 a.m. for homeroom. I figured I would be much happier once I found a position conducive to my livelihood, with something near my home, and a change of environment could do the trick.

After teaching at the alternative school for three years, I finally got the break I was looking for. I was hired to teach theater at a middle school near my house. I went from having a 55-minute drive to a 15-minute drive. It seemed like I'd paid my dues and everything was beginning to unfold like I was expecting. I thought the next 25 years would be a breeze.

The school year started off great. I was energetic and enthusiastic about my new position. However, the honeymoon phase ended quickly. Nine weeks into the school year, the principal needed to split my schedule and teach eighth grade social studies along with theater. Since the theater program was new to the school, I still had high expectations of myself on making sure the theater program was a success. With the added curriculum, I was afraid that I was not going to be able to live up to my own expectations. I was putting too much pressure on myself instead of going with the flow.

In the midst of the daily grind, Amanda and I checked off another box from our grocery list, and purchased a townhouse. I was fortunate to have a teaching job with benefits, along with a side bartending gig, so Amanda could enroll in the dental hygiene program. It was my understanding that I was doing everything I should be doing and should have been happy that I was "living the dream." I absolutely adored being around Amanda, but I was not happy. Amanda gave me additional support by purchasing resume paper so I could find my happiness. Amanda is a cheerful person and always lit up the room when she came in. Her personality was contagious, so there was no reason to be miserable. Why was I miserable? I was doing what I was supposed to be doing, wasn't I?

In this process, I slowly started forgetting who I was, and felt like a cog in the system. Everything became routine, like I was in a trance blindly going through the motions. The longer I gave myself to the system, the more frozen I became, losing myself in the process. The system conflicted with my beliefs, but it was something I was doing because I was made to believe it was right. It slowly overtook who I was and was no longer the same person as when I started the journey. I was entirely stuck in the daily grind, the displeasure and routine of being on the Gravitron. A student asked me what I wanted to be when I got old. I replied, "I'm still trying to figure that out."

The longer I was a teacher, the more lost I became with myself, the more distant I felt at home, and the further I felt from my purpose. I had mild anxiety on a regular basis, but I figured it was a part of life and something I should just learn how to deal with. I was not filling the role of the expectations I had for myself. I was not a disciplinarian and felt uncomfortable when I had to be, a situation I had way too often. I felt being a disciplinarian took a lot out of me and required me to tune in to negative energy, more than I was willing to accept. Unfortunately, I took the negative energy home with me, slowly encompassing my spirit. I knew a change was coming, but I did not know from where.

I loved being a teacher. However, I felt like I was limiting my potential and could reach a much broader audience than the 100 students I saw every year. If I was going to make a change in the world, I needed to do something more dynamic. I knew I needed to break free from the daily routine, and to step outside my comfort zone in order to do what felt right. I needed to be inspired and find something that would enable me to make a bigger impact on society. I had the desire to be a motivational speaker, but suddenly found myself in need of motivation. I did not know where to go or who to seek to pursue a career as a motivational speaker, but knew I would not find it if I did not make a change in my profession.

90% of life is just showing up. When your job becomes routine, simply performing tasks with your eyes closed, you risk becoming complacent and controlled by your circumstance. When you do not make any changes to your current situation, and remain content with your position, nothing in your life will change.

Building a Business

I met an acquaintance through one of my best friends, who worked in the financial services industry. After hearing a little bit about the company and earning potential, I decided to take a leap of faith and leave teaching after 5 years. The company had a loud message and I felt like this was an opportunity to reach as many people as possible. I was sold on the idea of running a private business with unlimited earnings potential, managing clients' wealth, and having complete control of my schedule. When I was younger, I loved being around money and dreamed of being an investment banker one day, but felt

I was never qualified to do so. This opportunity seemed like a great way to break into the industry.

First-year agents received exclusive training from the company. I could not get past the fact that we were learning insurance products versus investment options, many being masked as an investment vehicle, but figured it would be a gradual process before working our way up to sound financial investment. It was also suggested that we become extremely familiar with insurance products before moving onto securities since it required several other exams, which second and third year agents began studying. It seemed reasonable, and I was eager to learn how to build a business.

After finding my niche and working with school districts, I felt like I was building momentum in this business venture. I passed the initial securities exams, such as the Series 6 & 63 in order to suggest variable products our company was offering, but still had not learned about the stock market or other market conditions to look for, considering we were selling variable products. I was told I needed to pass the Series 7 & 65 in order to earn the designation as a financial advisor to suggest and sell stocks, so I brushed it aside considering my lack of credentials.

During the third year in the industry, I attempted to further my credentials and earn the title of financial advisor. After reading through the materials for the Series 7, I still did not feel I was credible enough to discuss current market conditions. The material was vague, and if I passed the exam, I did not feel I would be any better off than where I was before taking the exam. Even though I had the credentials to discuss the market as a "Financial Professional," it felt like I had more questions than answers. I decided to read the Series 65 materials to see if it would help. It did not. I had a hard time understanding that if I passed the Series 7 & 65, I would be able to call myself a financial advisor.

I did not feel competent enough to talk about the overall market conditions so I began losing interest in the industry. Shortly thereafter, I learned from another agent in the office that even with the credentials, advisors were prohibited from making discretionary trades or soliciting stocks on their behalf. We were only able to suggest products the company offered under their securities system. It did not feel right that we were limited on what we could suggest as investment vehicles, and somehow it was supposed to fit in clients' needs as to what was "suitable" for them.

The experience with the financial firm led to my initial phase of the awakening process. It was like the dark cloud that had been following me around suddenly lifted. The knot of anxiety that was deep in my chest was slowly beginning to unravel. It triggered the clarity I was looking for. The questions that were avoided over the years were answered all at once. I never felt comfortable working in the financial services industry. Everything I learned was new to me. I felt it was my obligation and duty to share with my clients any recent discoveries that would benefit them. I felt like a square peg in a circular system and could not assimilate with their culture.

I was able to last as long as I did because of the clientele I worked with. Thankfully, it was mostly harmless products that I felt comfortable selling, but it still was not ideal by any stretch of the imagination. It felt like a job I was simply tolerating for the sake of a paycheck. The value I gained from the experience was learning how to put a successful business together. The intensity of this alone was the reason I enjoyed the industry, and stayed for as long as I did. I did not mind the daily grind, and every new school district I landed felt like I was making a positive imprint on the lives of many. As soon as I learned my role would be limited, it was time to seek employment elsewhere. After committing my energy into the industry for nearly 4 years, it was time to focus on what I had been passionate about since I was kid: stock trading.

Investing in Yourself

If your place of employment makes you feel like are not serving your purpose, not in control of your situation, or like you are stuck on the Gravitron, leave. That will put you on the right path to freedom and happiness. Trust your intuition. It keeps you honest. Do not let others tell you how you should feel. You are an individual with unique personal qualities. With the abundance of time on your hands, and energy that is no longer being outsourced to a miserable work environment, you can use your newfound energy to seek ventures that feel right. You will begin to tap into your intuitive nature by trusting your instincts. Seek answers and guidance at all times.

I realized how much I used to read. I mostly read textbooks, articles, and other forms of literature that pertained to my profession. I began using my free time to search for meaning. I was fortunate to apply what I had learned from every job that I have had towards my own benefit. I would not be in the position I found myself in without these experiences. You need these detours to discover your true self. Not long after I checked out of my position with the financial firm, I began focusing on my number one investment: myself.

Setting up your own trading and retirement account is very rewarding, but can be risky if you do not do your own research. Becoming self-sufficient by setting up your own retirement account will provide you with "benefits" an employer will never be able to match. "Benefits" is an arbitrary term that has you undermining your potential when it comes to setting up your OWN benefits. Society has laid out before you that you need to have an employer that provides benefits in order to have the retirement you deserve.

You do not need a job that provides benefits, retirement, paid time off, etc. If you are perfectly healthy, use your able-bodied years to build your brand and establish your *own* benefits. You have been told your entire life to find a job/career that will provide you with benefits, retirement, and stability of income. When you focus on your own financial situation, you become more informed on what you should be doing in regards to retirement. It is not too difficult, and anyone can manage their own portfolio. By setting up your retirement account, you will not have to worry about compromising your health and well-being by locking yourself into a job for the next 30 years that you are no longer passionate about. If your end goal is to not have to work for anyone, then take the initiative today by not relying on an employer's benefits to keep you going. This takes the burden off the employer as well as yourself.

Setting up your own retirement and brokerage account is a very simple process. Choose a broker you feel comfortable with. Some brokers require a minimum amount of money to open an account. It just depends on how actively you plan on trading your portfolio and what your overall purpose is. I like to use E*TRADE as one of my trading platforms. They have great customer service and have many features when establishing a healthy portfolio. You can use the platform to establish a traditional or Roth IRA for retirement, and an individual brokerage account for liquidity of assets.

Since I cannot give financial advice, do your research when purchasing stocks. As Jim Cramer suggests, start with an index fund that matches the S&P 500. The stock ticker is: SPY. Simply log in to your trading account, type in the stock ticker: SPY, and make your purchase. I like to use the remaining funds and allocate to blue-chip stocks, such as Amazon (AMZN), Apple (APPL), Google (GOOGL), NVidia (NVDA), and Tesla (TSLA), for example. Distribute your portfolio amongst 10-15 stocks, varying in sectors (technology, health, auto, energy, retail, defense, etc.). Always keep cash in your portfolio so you can take advantage of buying on the dips. If the overall market happens to drop 20-25% over a short period of time, generally speaking, you are buying stocks 20-25% cheaper than they were days earlier. Take advantage of the dips instead of dwelling on the pullbacks. Pullbacks are common, so embrace them.

You can also establish your own health insurance through the healthcare marketplace, currently www.healthcare.gov You can also set up health insurance through your own personal business, even if you are independent. Always seek advice from your accountant, as we live in an ever-changing system.

Shifting Towards My Purpose

I am grateful for my experience in the financial services industry. I learned how the business world operates, and learned how to build my own business. I gained more than I lost from the experience. However, that experience could be avoided by focusing on what you are passionate about, while learning how to build your own business. You do not need to spend four years chasing your tail when you can make greater use of your time building your own business. You will enjoy the journey and process as your business plan is coming together, while at the same time learning how to develop a plan to benefit your audience.

During the journey, you will observe that everything happens for a reason. If I had stock trading experience prior to joining the financial services industry, there would have been a great chance that I would not have lasted four days, let alone four years. Many of the questions would have already been answered. I would have missed out on the chance to learn how to build a business, rather than figuring out how to create one on my own. Even though my time could have been allocated to learning how to build a business in a fraction of the time, I needed the experience to put myself in the right mindset in order to pave the way towards my purpose.

My initial passion in life became fulfilled after reallocating my energy into myself rather than an entity. The first thing I shifted my attention towards was the stock market. As I was in the midst of breaking free from the psychological prison I created for myself, after years and years of programming, I began reading literature that brought me value that would be further compounded for years to come. I read a stock trading book from a credible stock trader in the industry. I was so fascinated by his experience that I finished the book in two days. His book provided a lot of insight about the industry.

After reading his book and watching a few of his videos on YouTube, I decided to purchase his program. The stock trading program consisted of daily video lessons of stock market activity, multiple DVDs focusing on different areas of the stock market, and access to the trading floor chatroom. It was affordable, and much cheaper than college tuition. The value I received from the program exceeded my expectations and brought more value than what I received from any class I took in college.

Focus Your Energy on Your YOU

You are often glamorized by how great your company is and what they can do for you as long as you continue giving yourself to them. You might be in a position where you can continue furthering your education in your profession, adding more designations and credentials, and inevitably diluting what you can do for yourself in the process. By doing so, you are pulling time away from you, and placing your attention into your company.

You work when you are sick, pick up overtime when approached, and sacrifice your mental and emotional well-being in order to dedicate a big portion of your time, energy, and focus for a company or organization that would post your position for hire before your obituary hits the press. As you continue to push through any illnesses or temporary setbacks, your employer continuously reminds you how lucky you are to have *this* job. You have paid sick and vacation time, benefits, pension, and a 401k with employer-matching contribution up to X%. You frequently hear day in and day out, from your bosses, co-workers, family, friends, and acquaintances, how fortunate you are to work where you are working. You generally oblige, but cannot get past wondering why you are feeling down on yourself.

You are in the position you are in today because of the sacrifices you have made your entire life. Often you repeat the same habits and cannot figure out why you find yourself in the same situation over and over again. You regularly fill your quiet time with a distraction, something that becomes an escape from your everyday reality. Your awareness in the moment, or lack thereof, bounces around from one thing to another, for the entire day. You have never been taught how to *use* your mind. You need to practice how to use your attention and focus on one thing, and fully concentrate on that one thing for a long period of time. Make it become your habit and your lifestyle. A simple redirection of focus will help you shift gears towards your purpose.

Focus your awareness on yourself and what you can do to improve your situation just a little each day. When you become a better version of yourself by 1% each day, you have the potential to become 37 times greater than you were the previous year. Test the waters in different fields, applying your energy and focus into your goals. Work out daily, whether you are going to the gym, practicing yoga, or even just walking around your neighborhood. By doing so, you are stimulating your focus, as well as your mental and physical health. Turn off the television and social media platforms, and take the initiative to improve your situation. When you have a positive outlook on life, you will attract more positive into your life.

When you focus on your desires, and work towards your definite purpose in life, you will not need a defined benefits plan by your company. Investing in yourself will stretch much further when you reach the age of retirement. When you are working in something you are truly passionate about, then your work no longer becomes a chore, it becomes a hobby.

The average millionaire has seven sources of income. Working for yourself means you have the flexibility to control who, when, and where you work, even if it is tacked on to a 9-5 job. In the journey, you will collect additional streams of revenue, and build a retirement plan through accumulation of assets and wealth. You will not need to retire when you love what you do. By giving yourself all your focus and energy, you will be able to raise your frequency and vibration, and achieve higher levels as you progress through life.

The longer you focus on your vision and purpose in life, the more fulfilled you will become. You will not feel affected by the Monday grind. You will be excited when Mondays arrive. Mondays will present you with new opportunities that you can build from. Each experience becomes a building block into a new discovery throughout the journey.

Fulfill Your Desires

For most people, Monday is the least favorite day of the week. Almost everyone dreads Mondays. Everything is routine. It is like playing a character or performing a role on a daily basis. You can no longer separate your work character from your personal life character, as they slowly merged together as one. You have been conditioned to bring your work life home with you because of your daily habits. Your life became your work and your work became your life. The feeling is like you are trapped on the Gravitron without an exit strategy other than retirement.

If what you are doing right now is keeping you from fulfilling your desires, you need to reevaluate your position. When you are not effectively pursuing your purpose, you will continue to repeat the same patterns. In order to get to where you want to be, you need to take risks. Wayne Gretzky, the greatest goal scorer in NHL history, once said, "You miss 100% of the shots you don't take." Once you are able to break free from your current situation, it will feel like a weight has been lifted off your chest, like you are watching a balloon floating away. You have become the balloon who is no longer affected by the gravitational pull we call society. Your life will suddenly become very quiet as you become present in the moment.

How often do you spend time alone? Time is the most valuable asset you can have, and the cheapest. The sense of freedom you would feel without having to report to work and being told what to do by a boss would be a sense of independence you had not felt since you were a child. By spending time alone, you will learn how to discover your purpose. Create positive distractions that serve your purpose. All other forms of distractions inhibit your ability to achieve your greatest desires. The mindfulness in the present enables you to become fulfilled in your desires. You will never be fulfilled when you waste time with mindless activities.

Money does not buy happiness, nor will it make you feel fulfilled. Think about what makes you feel fulfilled. Is it material things like a car, expensive watch, rare collectibles, boat, etc.? If you had enough money to buy anything and everything you ever wanted, could you live the rest of your life and be happy? Remember when you were younger and the excitement you had when you purchased something you always wanted? Once you received this special item and enjoyed it for a few weeks, the novelty wore off and you begin searching for something else to fill the void. This trend will continue until you learn how to fulfil your life with your desires that will make you *happy*.

Too many people use social media to show the world how great they have it, particularly by flaunting material things. They are not sharing the reality behind the scenes of what their life is actually like. Even if they owned the luxury items depicted, there would still be a sense of emptiness inside. They are only showing these material things to feel validated. Receiving everything you ever wanted will still not provide you with fulfillment unless you enjoy the process of gaining your riches.

Fulfillment comes from within and it is up to you to decide what makes you happy. Finding fulfillment will lead to discovering your purpose in life. Once you discover your true purpose, establish a concrete plan, visualize what you are going to accomplish as if the vision is your reality. Feel the vision within you as your reality as if the version of you already exists. Upon doing so, your thoughts, imagination, feelings and aspirations will raise your frequency, ultimately manifesting into your desires. The universe will align itself to put you in a position of where you need to be.

Chapter Fourteen

LET THE RIVER FLOW

The River's Flow

One of our natural human instincts is survival. After an event takes place, it cannot be undone. You have to accept things for the way they are. How you respond or react is your natural survival instincts. The way you respond is derived from your subconscious mind. If the event is negative, your inner self comes out in its truest form. Your reaction can either be positive or negative. If you do not like how you respond, you have the power within you to reshape and reprogram your subconscious mind. A negative reaction is similar to attempting to reverse the natural flow of a river. The river has spent years and years carving its way downstream. Any disruption of the river's flow will create unforeseen obstacles. For example, if you create a dam to prevent the natural flow of the river from reaching its destination, you are simply delaying the inevitable. Through the process of erosion, the dam will deteriorate over time, creating more damage to the environment than building the dam itself. You cannot make a river flow in the opposite direction, and altering the natural dimensions of the river will prolong the inevitable. The flow of the river is constant, as well as the event that has already happened. It cannot be undone. As the river flows downwards like gravity intended, accept the events that took place in your life without resistance. Let them come naturally for you like the river's flow. When the event is negative, learn how to make the event work for you, not against you.

Oftentimes, we fail to listen and process new information. Our immediate reaction may not always be the best one. When something happens in your life, sit back and reflect on the event. What is the message the universe is sending? How can you grow and improve from this event that transpired? The event has already happened, and therefore cannot be changed. The only thing you can control is how you respond. Take time to digest new information rather than immediately reacting.

The universe works in a mysterious and beautiful way. Trying to control nature is the same as trying to control the universe. It cannot happen. You can only control how you respond to the universe as if you are directly communicating with it. You are interacting with the universe every day and may not even realize it. Your thoughts become your reality. If something bad happens and you get angry, you are attracting more bad things in your life, which will lead to more anger. Delay how you respond, and process new information as it comes to you. Be friendly with the universe and the universe will be friendly to you.

Gatlinburg, Tennessee, is one of my favorite places to visit. I love to take in nature, for its natural beauty, and I enjoy the benefits of what it has to offer. Whitewater rafting in Rifle River is one of the thrill-seeking activities I enjoy. The rapids are not so extreme that you feel unsafe, but it gives you enough adrenaline to feel the pull from the river. You are at the mercy of the river while you are rafting. If you fight and resist the flow of the river, the river will win every time. The best thing to do is surrender to the river and let it carry you downstream. You will be able to maneuver through the river, but ultimately it will carry you to your final destination.

If you attempt to fight against the river's natural flow, you are going to face a lot of resistance. The more you fight, the more tired you become. If you allow the battle to get you upset or angry, you will struggle more against the river's flow. By trying to paddle upstream, you are disrupting the universe's natural flow, the law of gravity. The same goes with life. We have all heard the expression "pick your battles." Most battles occur after the event has already taken place. Instead of trying to fight every battle, reflect on what message is being sent. Ask yourself, "Is this battle really important?" "Who am I battling with?" "What do I win or lose in this battle?" Oftentimes, when you engage in battle, you are protecting your ego, which is a made-up persona you created for yourself. When you give attention to a battle, you are taking your energy away from something that can be more constructive.

The majority of your external battles either come from a person or entity. If someone tries to engage in battle, the only thing you can control is how you respond. It is only a reflection of them, not you. It does not matter how right you are in the situation. You spend your energy on the person or the incident that does not deserve your attention, rather than directing it towards something beneficial that brings you more value. By removing the distraction from your life, you can focus on what really matters: YOU!

Building a Partnership

During my time in the financial services industry, I was able to take an in-depth look at how the industry operates. A college friend of mine was working with someone he thought was a trusted financial advisor. He was confident about his retirement account, because he felt that the money was in good hands. When I did a little research, I discovered that his financial advisor was not a financial advisor at all, and was only suggesting options that he would make a commission on, versus what was suitable for his clients. Whenever my friend would inquire about the stock market, his "advisor" would deflect, changing the subject to something he was able to discuss.

After sharing this information with my friend, he was appalled and immediately pulled money from his retirement account. During this time, he was estranged from his brother. Prior to their estrangement, they worked with the same financial representative. He did not want to let his brother live the next 30 years in an inferior portfolio when he could be in something that performed much better. My friend broke the ice and shared this information with his brother, and in doing so, they were reunited and reestablished their relationship.

While they were catching up after being estranged, they were eager to share with each other what they had learned. My friend was learning about stocks and stock options while his brother was investing in real estate. The two of them purchased a property together in a blind auction, strategizing together to build their wealth. The property was not what they had hoped for, and they learned a lot of tough lessons along the way.

In the meantime, I learned about a business opportunity using property in the short-term rental (STR) market with the use of a couple popular platforms. I had already turned my primary residence into a short-term rental as an additional source of income. I knew very little about the about the STR business, but it was something I became passionate about, and had early success in. I made minor adjustments to my townhouse to make it short-term rental friendly. I initially looked at the property as an additional source of income rather than being a destination paradise for travelers. I had a few good ideas early on, but was content with how the operation worked for the time being.

The interior was bland to say the least. The microwave had a broken handle, so I had to show guests how to use the needle-nose pliers to open the door. The rest of the appliances, old carpet, and the living room furniture were substandard. The new additions to my townhouse at the time included a dividing wall in the hallway, a door that separated the kitchen from the other side of the townhouse, a futon and TV stand in the makeshift living room, and a piece of art I received from a good friend, and hung above the bed.

Even with these substandard qualities, I was receiving 5-star reviews, mostly because I attempted to go above and beyond for my guests. In addition to the common items, I made sure they did not have to buy things they would only use for a few days, such as oil, spices, coffee, creamer, sugar, etc. before having to throw them away. I also provided my guests with eggs, water bottles, a waffle maker, and an air popcorn machine, but I knew I had a long way to go in order to make it superior to other short-term rentals in the neighborhood. After a successful first 2.5 months in October, November, and early December, I headed to Michigan for the holidays.

My parents were excited to hear the good news about short-term property business and I was excited to share my recent success with my friends. As I was hanging out with a friend, I received a booking for February. He inquired about the short-term property rental business and I was happy to share what I had learned. He liked hearing about this opportunity, so he shared this information with his brother, who was already renting houses on a monthly basis.

I planned on staying in Michigan for a week before returning home to Charleston. My dad was scheduled to have knee replacement surgery two days before I was scheduled to leave. After having knee-replacement surgery, I knew I could not leave my parents without my assistance. I decided that I would stay a bit longer and help around the house while he recovered. Also, with the snowy conditions, I did not want my mother outside in the blistering cold taking out the trash, shoveling snow, or any other chores my dad would have done. It would have been selfish for me to leave.

Since I was in town longer than expected, I was able to further discuss the short-term rental business with my family and friends. Having it constantly on my mind enabled me to brainstorm and visualize ways to improve my personal property in the process. I returned home after a six-week stay in Michigan, and had an epiphany. It dawned on me while I was in Michigan that people travel to get the vacation feel of being in a different city. My townhouse did not have the vacation feel that it should. It felt like a home or an apartment like in any other state, and the only difference was where the townhouse was located. It was very similar to my parents' home: brown, with neutral colors throughout. I wanted my home to resemble paradise, and to make my guests feel like they were on vacation.

After returning to Charleston, I could not get settled in my own home. Nothing felt right. I had several awakening experiences while in Michigan, and felt as if my house was no longer a reflection of the person I had become. I needed to update the interior of my house to resemble how I felt. I was willing to challenge myself and see what I was capable of achieving. Instead of living in fear of what could go wrong, I lived in anticipation of what could go right.

Up until this point, I was incompetent when it came to construction or interior design. The most that was expected of me was changing a light bulb or changing out the battery in the smoke alarm. My entire life I was made to believe I was not capable of anything that involved using tools of any kind. Upon my awakening, my belief system began to shift. I remembered many scenarios that made me believe I was not able to perform certain tasks, so I had to reprogram and retrain my subconscious mind. I learned that my limitations were self-inflicted because I placed value on what I was told I was not capable of doing rather than telling myself, "I can." I got tired of waiting around, and began to challenge my competence and capabilities, and so the journey began...

Never Give Up

I could not get comfortable in my own home and nothing felt natural. I felt like I was being pulled to make a change. I felt impatient and had this sudden burst of energy, and knew my frequency did not match my environment. In order to match my frequency with my surroundings, like the natural flow of a river, I listened to the universe and made a significant change. Fortunately, it was a slow season for short-term rentals, so I had a week to begin the transformation in my living room before the next guest was scheduled to arrive. I wanted to experiment with my side of the townhouse before remodeling the STR side. Without much direction, I went to the hardware store, bought painting supplies, and picked out a paint color that matched my frequency. I was attracted to brighter, earthier colors, so I chose a bright blue color. Since I live about 6 miles from the ocean, I wanted my place to resemble an environment where I am always happy – the beach!

I moved all the furniture to the center of the living room and began to paint. I did not know if I had the right supplies, or if it was going to be messy, if I had enough paint, or if the color would look good. It did not matter. I was ready to learn on the fly. As I was nearing the end of the paint job, I was ready to make another significant change to the living room. I had wanted hardwood floors instead of carpet my entire life, but always found myself in a place that had carpet. Heading into my 38th birthday, I was ready to have hardwood floors for the first time.

After the paint job was finished, I did not hesitate one bit and began ripping up the carpet. I purchased the materials for the new floor and began to research how to install it. I heard horror stories years earlier from co-workers installing hardwood floors, who recommended hiring someone to install them for you. I realized that when someone says something concerning to me, they are expressing their limitations, not mine. I felt I was capable of achieving any task with the proper research. I was no longer going to let someone else's incapabilities affect my position. Suddenly, I felt like I was capable of anything. If I was not competent enough, I would figure it out as I would go along. I figured, what is the worst that could go wrong? You do not know unless you try and you could be amazed at what you are capable of achieving once you give yourself permission. If you fail, so what? There is no such thing as failure as long as you do not quit. Every failed experience is a learned lesson of what not to do.

On Saturday morning, on my 38th birthday, I was about to attempt something I never thought possible – installing new flooring in the living room. My goal was to finish the entire floor on my birthday. I had a few minor hiccups along the way, but mission accomplished! It was very inspiring to see what I was able to create. I learned so much during the first week of this journey, that it left me excited to see what I was capable of achieving next. I had a whole house to get to and I was just getting started. I hung all the new décor on the wall and it really began to feel like being on vacation. I changed the entire scenery, removing reminders from my past, in order to keep moving forward.

The following week I did the same exact thing to my bedroom. I moved all the furniture out into the living room and began the same process all over again. The living room had a beach theme, so I made the bedroom look like a Charleston theme. Since it was my side of the townhouse, and not the rental side, I had the flexibility to be as experimental as I wanted to be. The transition between the two rooms was perfect! It was exactly what I had imagined. I used the leftover floor planks and installed them into the kitchen before moving on to the bathroom. I was in a constant state of FLOW.

Within a month, I had completely remodeled and redecorated my half of the townhouse. I had a vision on what the STR would become, but had to intermittently work between guests, so I focused my attention on my backyard instead. Within a week, I took my un-inviting, dreary backyard, and made it into an oasis. I transformed it with brighter colors, giving it a beach themed feel as well. My buddy came by and asked if I had purchased new pavers for my yard. I said, no, I just power-washed them. My friend, who is not particularly animated in his responses, was amazed by the transformation. This made me feel great, knowing that I was on the right path.

Similar to the transformation of the living room, I created a beach-theme in the backyard. I created a mini beach, added an orange tree, painted the wooden fence white, and made the rest of the yard inviting. It was great to see the wildlife contrast against the white fence. Every day I felt like I was watching the nature channel with the lizards running around and chasing each other, while sitting back in my mini beach and meditating. My energy was being revitalized and restored, and I was enjoying the process.

I was sharing these makeovers with my friends and family, including the friend who had just rekindled his relationship with his brother. They were both eager to create something with me and everything was feeling natural and moving together smoothly, so we decided to work out a partnership. At this point, I felt like I was capable of any fixer-upper project, so I was ready to jump in and get started. We ended up finding the perfect property within our budget, a condo in a nearby neighborhood, and decided to recreate the theme I had when renovating my home. It was definitely a fixer-upper; however, my drive, focus, and motivation were at their highest levels, and I could not wait to get started.

We closed on the condo on April 20th, and began renovating on April 21st. I pulled my attention away from my STR in order to focus on this new property with the brothers. I shared my vision with them, and conveyed the plan with the condo. They were all in from the start. At the time, this partnership seemed like a match made in heaven, and as natural as the river flow. They had the equity to fund the project, while I had the time to research the property, renovate, and had experience running a successful STR. Since I was a Super Host, we agreed we would hold the property under my platform during prime season in order to draw more attention, then shift over to a joint account when the season slowed down.

The brothers and I agreed to use the same color scheme and

theme I had for my townhouse. I began painting early that morning, and by 10 p.m. that night, I was ready to call it a night. I had accomplished more in one day than I did in a week at my house. I painted the bedroom, kitchen, dining, and laundry room, along with laying the new floors from the kitchen through the dining room.

On day 2, I finished the floors in the laundry and painted the bedroom. While I was painting the bedroom, I decided to add a little humor and paint my name on the wall. Upon sharing this with the brothers, I was scolded for "too much yellow!" I was in disbelief at their reaction. I thought they would laugh it off. I was confused because we agreed upon the color. I did not think much of it and continued with the project as reflected in my vision.

On day 3, I began a project I dreaded – the bathroom. The bathroom was in terrible shape. My brother gave me numerous much-needed cleaning tips. The vanity was disgusting so it had to be replaced. Simply cleaning the entire bathroom, along with the new paint job, took the entire day. I was proud of my accomplishments and sent pictures to everyone in my family. They were all supportive of the work I had done thus far. However, I became discouraged when my business partners failed to acknowledge the transformation. Their response, or lack thereof, was comparable with the paint job in the bedroom. I figured they were either busy or just expected it of me. I knew it was not the expectation of my family, because they knew this was all new to me. It began to feel like I was being treated as an employee rather than a partner. However, I was not going to let this faze me. Either way, I ignored their lack of interest and kept moving forward.

I completed the project in 16 days, not counting the days I drove around the state to look for furniture, décor, and other essential items to make the condo a running business. I was proud that we had the property listed by May 16th. Mission accomplished. Even though the property was listed, there were still plenty of other things that needed to be worked on between guests, but nothing too significant.

Ripples Become Riptides

Our STR got off to a great start. We earned our first booking within hours of being listed. We continued to earn bookings throughout the summer, just as we'd expected. Since the STR was under my platform, I was responding to all inquiries, guest concerns, etc., and made myself readily available to put out any fires when needed. The monies earned were immediately transferred into our joint account. As the money was coming in, I began to notice a few things that were very unsettling.

In order to save our property money, I took on the responsibilities of cleaning after every guest, performing any repairs that were within my capabilities, and other guests' issues. The money was to be used to pay the bills and reimburse expenses we put into the condo. I observed a lot of the money being withdrawn without my consent, and was told it was going to expenses they had put into the condo before I was being reimbursed. After prime season ended, we earned 5-star reviews from every guest. By October, it was time to put the property into a joint account like we had originally agreed.

After the property was listed under my STR for 5 months, from May–September, I reminded the brothers that we needed to switch profiles per our agreement, in order to shift the responsibilities from myself over into a joint effort. I asked them to create the joint account, which surprisingly they were reluctant to do. After I said I would be delisting the condo from my platform, they responded by saying they never agreed to this transition and ordered I relist the property under my platform once again. After several messages and a phone call, they created a STR profile under our agreed upon platform and relisted the property under their personal account, which we called our joint account.

The partnership continued to be shaky from there. It seemed like I was paddling up a river with one paddle. The signs of the universe kept pulling me away, but I chose to ignore the signals. We had several disagreements about petty things, and could not seem to gain a consistent flow. I could feel the energy shifting from positive to negative. I made compromises with myself along the way. Even though I was passionate about the condo, after putting all my focus and energy into the property, since it was my first fixer-upper renovation project, my mission was accomplished. I had proven to myself that the condo was a success after earning glowing reviews.

I took a step back and passed the baton over to my partners and let them assume control of the STR platform. I figured since I had learned from personal experience what worked and what did not, this would be a good experience for them to manage the property and handle inquiries and guest engagements. With taking the path of least resistance, this enabled me to refocus my attention back to my townhouse, since it was still my baby. Aside from some minor adjustments, I pretty much ignored my personal STR and was ready to give it the attention it deserved.

After creating a Charleston and beach theme on my half of the townhouse, as well as the condo, it was time for me to create a similar feeling for my personal short-term rental. After a successful spring and summer, it was a slow season once again. Even though my property did well, I was determined to use the energy and focus I put into the condo, and reallocate it to my property. I found myself getting inspired from all sources, and visualized what the townhouse could soon become. My townhouse went through a complete make-over by late February. I started getting bookings months in advance. I was able to charge more per night because of the new look. This was the most rewarding feeling when putting my personal STR together. Everything was moving perfectly with my townhouse and I was motivated to see what we could accomplish with the condo.

The condo had been listed under my partners' names since October. I continued to play a key role in the process, handling the cleaning responsibilities until we hired a cleaner in early January. I began to notice some odd behavior. They liked being in control, and gained energy by trying to eliminate any role that I had with the condo, especially after hiring a cleaner. Upon hiring a cleaner, the partners and I discussed when the cleaner would be allowed access to the condo. The partners emailed the cleaner to let her know what her accessibility rights would be. They also mentioned in the same email that I would no longer be in the condo for any reason. Being undermined in the email should have been enough evidence to walk away from the partnership, but it seemed abrupt and I thought the relationship could be fixed. The pattern of behavior that led up to that point was enough to recognize I was not part of the river's flow and was actually stuck in a riptide.

After giving my business partners the freedom to control the STR platform, they demonstrated a pattern of manipulation and deception that I was hoping I could resolve. It was one thing after another, to the point where it became hysterical. Their deceptive practices continued to build, leaving me to wonder what their intent was. It seemed like they were trying to cut me out of the operation; however, my family and friends were saying I was just being paranoid. Maybe I was, but from an intuitive standpoint, I felt like my awareness was rising, and the partnership felt like it was leaving me with more questions than answers.

As we were heading into prime season, I noticed a few days on our calendar were blocked. After I asked them why, they said they'd listed the property under a different STR platform, and said it was something that was never discussed. I agreed, it was never discussed, therefore the property needed to be removed from the account. After they refused to delist the property, we agreed that the additional platform would be beneficial as long as our joint email was being used, and the money was being transferred directly into our joint account.

The signs from the universe kept pulling me away from this partnership, but I was curious to see how this pattern of behavior would play out from an educational standpoint and knew that it would provide greater perspective. I figured this experience would eventually protect me from future business endeavors, and that I'd learn how other people's character and integrity played out when there was money involved.

In early March, I noticed the calendar was blocked once again. Upon inquiring about the dates, they mentioned they were coming down to make repairs, and update and redesign our condo. At this point, I was fine with whatever they envisioned because it would be a new learning experience for me as well, and we needed some sort of camaraderie in our partnership. They wanted to repaint the place, which I was not too fond of, but I offered to assist. I was obligated to agree because it was two against one. I lost interest at this point because it felt like a constant upstream battle without a paddle. After helping them repaint the living room, they said they did not need me there and that they would take care of the rest without me.

When you are experiencing ripples turning to waves, a storm is coming. There is a need for full transparency and open conversation in order to preserve a partnership and maintain a relationship. When you are constantly battling with someone, and needing to control every situation, it eventually will become a part of you. It is better to let go, and not hold onto what would have been. You will not be able grow unless you stop repeating the past.

When the brothers completed the condo, I anticipated a change of temperament. They created something they were proud of, and I had already lived out the experience of my creation. When they left, they asked me to remove the trash and furniture left behind in the breezeway. One of the items was the coffee table from the living room. They insisted we did not need the coffee table, as well as the other furniture items that were removed because it created "clutter." They also gave away the bamboo table in the bedroom. Just about everything was rearranged from how I'd had it, including the location of the coffee pot, waffle maker, and pots and pans in the cupboards. It was like they were trying to undo any trace of my imprint. All I could do was laugh when I saw this.

After the first guest checked out, the cleaner noted that the laundry basket was left in the living room. The cleaner gave the impression that the guest had trashed the place, until I noted that the guest likely used the laundry basket as a makeshift coffee table. At this point, I expressed the need for a coffee table; however, both of my partners said it was not necessary.

This condo was an uphill battle from the start. Whenever it felt like we were making progress, an event would put us back in the same place we'd started. Instead of getting frustrated, try to take each experience for what can be gained, looking for the positives. From a universal perspective, there did not seem to be any synchronicity with the condo, nor the partnership, and some of the events seemed to be out of our control, like the universe was communicating to us. The good news was that we were very close to having paid back all our expenses, and prime season was upon us. It was only a matter of time before we were in the green. Then an unfortunate incident occurred.

About a month later, a guest emailed us and said the AC was not blowing cold air. Unfortunately, the AC unit needed to be replaced. That set us back another $2,100, but luckily we were booked through May and knew the incoming revenue would pay off what was owed and we could finally set our sights on being in the green.

184 | FIND YOUR YOU

In the meantime, when I arrived at the condo to see if there was anything I could do to jump start the AC unit, I observed the guest using the dining room chairs as a makeshift console table in the bedroom for their luggage, and using another chair as an end table in the living room. Again, after sharing these discoveries, the brothers claimed that they never said that we did not need a coffee table. This was one of many lies, but at least this time this lie was less than a month old, so it was easy to go back and trace it from their texts. Instead of ignoring this lie, like I did with many lies from the past, I sent them four screenshots from texts where they said we did not need a coffee table in the living room. I was hoping they would see from my perspective the lack of trust and communication I had with them. Unfortunately, their response was, "You must have too much free time on your hands. I thought I said it but I might have said it in my head."

After taking care of the furniture debacle, we had a successful May which enabled us to pay off the AC unit expense, with a positive outlook as we were heading into prime season. What happened next could have not have been any clearer that the universe was trying to tell us something.

I had a phenomenal review from my own STR. Everything seemed to be shifting to the positive. After the rocky start, possibly due to the financial concern wearing on the partners, it seemed like our minds would be at ease as soon as we became profitable. I shared the review with my partners and said we could get reviews like this if they allowed me run the condo how I operated mine. This was similar to how we operated the condo when it was under my own platform when we first started. They were hesitant and said they did not want to address any changes at this time. After this last form of resistance from them, the unthinkable happened and the universe responded accordingly.

I received a text early the next morning from the partners that the city had sent us a letter forcing us to delist our property. We all thought the property was located in the township, but it turned out it was located on the border of city limits. We were forced to delist the property as a short-term rental. We had two options at this point: either we could rent out the property for a few years and wait for it to increase in value and sell for a larger profit, or immediately sell the property. I wanted to hold onto the property since we were still able to rent it out for more than twice the operating expense, but they demanded we sell. Even though we needed all three signatures in order to sell, I felt obligated to sell. If we kept the property, I would have to continue with this partnership that was steering me away from my purpose. Had I held on to it, it would have been my ego wanting to keep the property until we turned a significantly larger profit.

I was no longer willing to continue the partnership when I could be focusing my efforts and energy on something that would bring greater value. Since it is impossible to multitask, my energy and attention were being absorbed by this property, when it could have been redirected into something greater. There were plenty of chances to make this partnership work, but the universe had a better plan for me. I was grateful for that experience, but it was a time to move on to the next adventure of my life and follow the flow of the river.

We sold the property within three days of listing it. We sold it for $14,000 more than we'd purchased it for. I expected to receive a percentage of the proceeds, but received a letter from them insisting there was no profit after selling the property. They gave several reasons why I would not be compensated. I could have argued and fought them over this, taken them to court, etc., but at this time in my life, I was ready to move on. The amount of time and energy I would have put back into the situation would have been like paddling upriver, preventing myself from moving forward. In the end, after spending the first 6 months of my time renovating, repairing, decorating and cleaning the condo 40+ times at no cost prior to hiring a cleaner, I walked away with $0.00, but the experience was invaluable.

What you put out in the universe will always come back for you in another shape or form. The law of compensation will reward those who earn it, and take away from those who do not. Just because you were not compensated as expected, does not mean you will not ever receive. You will receive what you've earned in another form. The opposite happens when you take. There is no such thing as a free meal. If you take something that was not earned, the universe will respond accordingly.

Follow the messages the universe is continuously sending you.

When you choose to ignore these messages, you will repeat the same patterns over and over. This is a clear example of thoughts becoming reality. When you are living in the past of the previous days' struggles, future events will unfold similarly, in another shape or form. Even when you are trying to manifest your thoughts into a positive outcome to become your reality, you are working with external forces that are against your control. In this scenario, simply set your vision aside for another partner, another rental property, or another experience for a different day. Do not let the same patterns repeat or else you will be trapped in your own thoughts.

Feel Rewarded from Within

Oftentimes, you find yourself in a struggle with your ego. You think it is your YOU that is being attacked or betrayed, so your immediate instinct is survive and protect your ego. Your reaction is to set boundaries for yourself, and so the battle ensues. You want to be treated the same way you treat others. Therefore, your initial instinct should be to understand their perspective. This behavior is only a reflection of them, not you. If you respond in an effort to protect your ego, it becomes a reflection of yourself. You will find that these behaviors repeat because you are continuously protecting your ego. The best thing to do in this circumstance is to walk away so the behavior does not become a part of you. By walking away, you are able to put all of your energy and effort into something else that will bring you fulfillment and further value.

We all like to be financially compensated for the work we do. This means we become programmed to work for money, and to be paid for the work we have done. You are willing to trade your time for money, leading you to believe that the only value you get from the job is through financial compensation. This is the wrong mindset to have. The universe is always working with you through the law of compensation. Your efforts will always be compensated, through various forms.

The law of compensation works when you are capable of going above and beyond what you expect. So many have the mindset, "It's not my job," and therefore refuse to assist when available. If you are capable of lending a helping hand, even though it is not part of your job description, then it IS your job. As Napoleon Hill states, "The man who does more than he is paid for will soon be paid for more than he does." When you are going above and beyond expectations, you are raising your frequency and vibration in the process. What goes out must always come in. This is how the law of compensation works. Whatever you put out in the universe will come back to you.

When you send out the message of lack, you confirm with the universe that you require less by ingraining insufficiency in your mind. You will continue to work for money until you realize that the real value is from what you gained internally. Plan as if you have all the time in the world regardless of your age. So many people feel when they are 26, 35, 45 or even 60, that the best years of their life have gone by. People are living longer today. If you took any of those age brackets, just know it does not take a lifetime to be successful. Each year comes with experience. It is what you put into those years that matters. Success comes with a strategy and the intention of achieving your plan.

Do not set out to achieve only a tangible goal, because you will lose out on what the value of the experience brings. If you keep sitting back and reflecting on what is owed to you, you will live in the past and lack will be at the forefront of your mind. If someone asked me if I would have been better off receiving what is "owed" to me without having this experience, I would have taken the experience over financial gains every single time. Money is replaceable. Experience is infinite. Once you get to a certain point in your life, the amount of money you have becomes pedestrian, but your experience will live on forever. Your experience is your foundation and becomes a building block to achieve bigger and greater things. Each experience prepares you for what is to come. The goal is not to get caught up in what is owed to you. You do not need to live your life quantifying your achievements though material things. Happiness and fulfillment are achieved from within. Whether you are "succeeding" or "failing" is arbitrary and based on someone else's standards. Do what you love doing because you enjoy the process and the journey. Do not get caught up in the immediate outcome and become an observer in your journey instead.

We have all had people in our lives who have betrayed us. Often, we do not learn our lesson and fall back into the same pattern of deception and betrayal. Some might say it is the nature of the beast. Continuously drawing attention to someone that is gaslighting you only attracts more negative attention that drains your energy. While you are reminding yourself that you do not want these negative people in your life, you are really responding to the universe that you want more of this in your life. The universe does not hear what you do not want, it only attracts more of what you do not want by giving it the undesired attention. A message to the universe of what you do not want is negative thought and cannot coexist. Instead of saying, "I don't want a bad business partner," say, "My new business partner is going to be open-minded and be a lot of fun to work with." Always focus on the positive and the universe will respond accordingly.

A fish becomes vulnerable to being captured when it travels upstream to lay its eggs. The fish's pattern becomes predictable, even jumping out of the water as it tries to climb a waterfall, becoming prey to bears and people. The fish's pattern is its nature. It is all it knows how to do. As you continue to struggle upstream, you are taking the path of most resistance. The more you fight against the current, the more vulnerable you will be. As your energy is being drained, you become susceptible to similar occurrences by finding yourself in the same situations over and over again. As you live in fear for what could go wrong, you are lowering your frequency to its lowest form.

When Albert Einstein was asked if this is a friendly universe or a mean universe, he said we live in a friendly universe. The universe is constantly sending you messages that will protect you. You cannot control what happens in your life, you can only control how to respond. Instead of entertaining something negative, give attention to things that bring you joy and happiness. Show gratitude for what has happened, rather than being angry and resentful. When you show gratitude for what has happened, the universe will respond more positively. Having the right attitude is what makes all the difference. You are in control of choosing your attitude.

Become an observer of the universe and reflect on your situation. Ask yourself what can be learned from this experience. What is your mission? I discovered my purpose after the universe redirected me on what seemed to be a few unsatisfying and unfulfilling business attempts. When you are not fulfilled, it is time to reflect on the journey and decide where you need to pivot. Experience equals success. There is no such thing as failure when you attempt a work or business venture. Failure is a mindset, and most people fail to even take the first step. The fact that you are taking the first step determines the journey towards success has already taken place.

By taking each event in stride, whether it is positive or negative, the way you respond is what you will continue to attract. Trying to change the event with your actions would be similar to trying to change the flow of the river. Once the event has happened, it has happened. Do not give it any more of your time or energy. Do not become a fish and take the bait. Just let the river flow and continue following your path that leads to your purpose.

Look at every opportunity as an experience that can be gained. When you are able to provide people less fortunate than you with compensation, your inner self and spirit will glow. Your aura will be prominent and people will recognize it when you walk into a room. Your energy and your spirit will be felt by those around you, and their presence will hold greater value than can ever be paid back through financial compensation.

CHAPTER FIFTEEN

THE JOURNEY TO FINDING YOUR YOU

You were placed in this world with a special gift. You are unique in your own way, unparalleled to anyone. You are not a one-dimensional being cut from the same cloth. You began your journey as a free spirit when you entered into this world. You had the imagination and creativity adults did not have. As you were expanding your imagination, you experimented with your ideas and discovered what worked and what did not work. During your early years, you were programmed for what society viewed as normal. Your parents, churches, and schools expected you to behave and cooperate a certain way, starting the process of putting your YOU in a box. Slowly, it absorbed into your subconscious, where it became your current YOU: a thick shell called your ego.

The conditioning of your current state began at birth. You were a sponge and absorbed everything around you. You were influenced from every environmental factor, such as the house you grew up in, the schools you attended, and the groups you associated with. Propaganda is strategically placed throughout your life in several forms: TV, across various social media platforms, YouTube ads, billboards and advertisements in your neighborhood, and the habits in your culture that became your customs. These factors control the mind and how you think.

Culturescape

Wherever you are from, you are taught what to think based on your culturescape. Whether you live in a large or small city, another country, or an indigenous tribe in Australia or Africa, your culturescape is what forms your thoughts and belief system. It is manmade. It is all around you and programs you. Your daily routines, beliefs, and other ideas come from your culture, including parents, churches, and teachers telling you how to be.

Ask yourself the following questions: Who am I? What am I passionate about? What do I desire? Where do my beliefs come from? What excites me? Question everything around you. Is the feeling natural? Most likely, up until this point, your information has come from other beings teaching you how to conform to your society's structural standards. Your new thoughts may become dismissed because they do not fill the role or standard of how someone else was taught. This does not make you wrong. It makes you curious. Build on your curiosity by expanding it even further. You will gain wisdom from your own personal experience.

Think about the things you are expected to do. You are expected to go to school, attend church, stand for the pledge of allegiance, change class when the bell rings, listen to your elders, and live inside the rules. These rules were created by people just like you and me, not anyone smarter than you. You are told to live inside these parameters that limit you. You are an infinite being with potential, not intended to be imprisoned within these walls created for us.

Your experiences make up the person you are. No two people are alike, even if you are a twin. Your perspective is adapted to your experiences. When you recognize these experiences in an event that occurs, you will say it was a coincidence. There are no coincidences. They are messages being transmuted to fit your belief system. The "coincidental" event matched your current frequency and vibration, which seemed like a coincidence. When you have certain thoughts, you will attract certain messages. When you continue repeating daily activities, jobs, habits, etc., you will see them occur in your daily life as if you were stuck on the Gravitron, as they make up your belief system.

When something bad happens, you may think the world is against you. Events such as a breakup, failed business, traffic violation, or waiting in line at the post office or DMV are all examples of events that will keep you trapped in your own mind. When your thoughts become your reality, you can expect to repeat similar events in your life until you start changing the way you think. When you start to believe there are opportunities outside these boundaries, you will begin to experience a new reality that has manifested from your imagination, separating you from the followers. The majority of the population is conditioned on how to think. When you feel odd or out of place, or something does not make sense, it is ok. It is your ego trying to make sense of it all. Your natural self is unaffected unless your ego imposes it on your nature. Being unique makes you one of a kind, and by noticing this about yourself, you become more aware.

I have had many acquaintances, but very few friends. I felt like I could not fit in with the rest of the crowd, because everything felt artificial and fake to me. When friends would purchase a car stereo system or rims for their car, I always thought that it was a waste of money, only to see my twin brother purchase a sound system for his car. I thought money could be better spent on things you actually need that would enhance your life. There is no need to be like everyone else. There needs to be only ONE of YOU!

When you are in a school, an office, at a sporting event, or out in the general public, notice how the majority of the population appears asleep at the wheel and going through the motions as though they have time to fill their day as they casually stroll along without a purpose. Some people are so engaged within their own subgroup that they do not even see the rest of the world around them. For the most part, the ones who are separate from the rest of the population, who do not seem to fit in, are born leaders trying to assimilate with the rest of the population, until they discover their true identity and purpose. I found myself as part of this group for the majority of my life, trying to fit in and be a follower with the rest of society. Whenever I tried to be an "adult" and conform to a "profession," I felt like I was being pulled by the wrist, giving me a mild case of anxiety, losing myself in the process. But how did I get here?

The Awakening

While I was questioning everything around me, looking for answers, a book manifested into my lap. It was exactly what I had been looking for. Up until this point, I had only read books that pertained to my career, most of which were study materials assigned to me for academics or my profession. I needed a book to continue expanding my mind and kept asking "what else" is out there.

The book, *Outwitting the Devil* by Napoleon Hill, was my first glance at achieving spiritual awakening, without even knowing what a spiritual awakening was. The book was slightly confusing for the first two chapters, but something deep inside told me to keep reading. When I began the third chapter, everything started to come together. It dawned on me that my entire belief system was being programmed by how I was raised, how I was told to think, and the environment I grew up in. These factors influenced how I was made to think.

As Alan Watts states, "There is no such thing as things." I discovered my belief system was phony and artificial. Everything that I thought mattered in life became irrelevant. The reality was that every day I woke up and got ready for work, I was pushing someone else's agenda and conforming to others' belief systems. Everything we have been taught has been made up over time. Society has been programming us, instead of teaching us how to think for ourselves. Jobs you are expected to take, the institution of marriage, social status by owning things that do not matter are all made up to control how you think.

During the initial phase of an awakening, you will feel like you have been looking at the world through a tinted window, and suddenly the window is rolled down and you can see everything much clearer. The next thing you need to do is walk outside and explore what you are seeing. The world will start to feel new to you now that you are seeing it through a different lens: your lens. Discover what you have been missing from this world. You will gain new experiences that are right in front of you. You will begin to create. The experiences you had before will no longer feel the same; they will appear artificial and made up.

While you are beginning the phases of your awakening, you will want to learn more about the truth of your YOU. You will reflect on what is important to you. Your desires will soon manifest because of your newfound faith, greater than any religious faith. It will become authentic. While you are discovering your true purpose, you will continue to have new awakening experiences as you unravel old belief systems.

You will not experience a full awakening all at once. You will continue to untangle more and more of your current belief systems, recalling certain memories that were hardwired in your brain, rewiring how you were told to think, little by little. During this phase, you begin to reprogram, recode, or recondition yourself to form a new belief system. Your intuitive nature becomes significantly stronger each day while you start to observe the universe inside you. You will feel more connected to the universe, and become more inspired upon discovering who you are. You will identify how we are all connected, and that the people you attract in your life are little pieces of you. You will begin to realize that there is no such thing as luck, because you will be following the signals the universe sends you, aligning you on your path; outsiders will see it as "luck."

The journey to discovering your true purpose has many advantages. You learn to put your ego aside, and truly examine the events that are happening around you. Instead of acting as a victim when something bad happens to you, reflect back and ask the universe why this event happened. What can be gained from this experience? You will start to feel these messages as little nudges to redirect you towards your true purpose. If you choose to ignore these messages, you will continue repeating the same patterns in your life, one after another. People who dwell on negative thoughts and emotions will also become imprisoned into those thoughts and will repeat events until they break free from the Gravitron.

We All Come from One Source

We are all connected. Simply put, going back to the Big Bang Theory, we all originated from stardust. Since we all came from the same "bang," we are connected one way or another. You will start to notice other people in you. As the Golden Rule states, treat others how you want to be treated. In doing so, you are treating people as you want yourself to be treated. If you are mean to others, you want others to be mean to you. Your actions are a reflection of yourself, not a reflection of what others say about you. When someone makes mean comments about your job, the car you drive, or even your physical appearance, they are projecting themselves onto you. Others projecting onto you is them wanting something they see in you that they do not have.

You become a part of everything around you, including your environment. You are where you are today because of the choices you made leading up to this point. The conversations you hear also become a part of you. If you hear a conversation that was not intended for you, it becomes a part of you for being in its presence.

Being a substitute teacher puts me in a position to overhear conversations without even trying. One day, I overheard a conversation between two young ladies being harassed on social media. They were stressing about what someone else had said about them and could not figure out what they had done to deserve this type of scrutiny. Upon hearing their comments, I felt the need to say something. I approached the two young ladies, and said, "It's not a reflection of you, it's a reflection of them." My comments stuck with them, as I could see their minds become at ease. They thought it over, and said, "Oh. Yeah. You're right!" before brushing it off. The burden of the comments no longer affected them, and seeing their immediate peace of mind is the reason why I love doing what I do.

You are beautiful, regardless of what others think. When someone calls you a name, attacking your appearance or your character, they are only wanting something you have – freedom of individuality and expression. They are not free because they are trapped in their own idea of what they should be: their ego. Regardless of your socioeconomic status, race, creed, etc., you are unique and special, different than anyone else. Your purpose is different from someone else's. No two snowflakes are the same, neither are two people. When you begin to see the universe inside of you, and have a higher sense of connectivity, you will become a major part of bringing unity throughout the world.

Reaching Your Purpose

When I was younger, I was a substitute teacher, aspiring to become a full-time teacher. My ego made me feel I had more to prove because I was not a regular classroom teacher yet. At the time, I was embarrassed to *only* be a substitute teacher. It meant that I had more work to do to become a full-time teacher. When I met someone new, I usually identified myself as a bartender rather than substitute teacher. Now, after being a full-time teacher, I love the fact that I am a substitute teacher. It is the best job in the world. I get to bounce around from school to school, classroom to classroom, and use the opportunity to make a change in someone's life. With the understanding that 85% of families are dysfunctional, I get to use the opportunity to influence and inspire thousands of kids throughout the year.

How do you get to your purpose? Experiment. Fail, and fail often, but never give up. As mentioned before, Thomas Edison learned 10,000 different ways not to invent the incandescent lightbulb. As Denzel Washington stated, "To get something you never had, you have to do something you never did." Break down the walls and barriers keeping you locked up. When you stop trying to become what other people want you to be, it opens up a world of freedom that you would have never imagined existed.

When I was growing up, I always felt the need for approval and validation from my family, friends, and even my colleagues. I was afraid to fail, so I took minimal risks. Being told "no" was scary to me. I wanted to be an actor or rapper, but I was afraid of the criticism that came with the risk; being told it was impossible did not help the way I thought, either. This paranoia in the back of my mind always seemed to linger. It felt like the auditions were going to break me, so I made compromise after compromise before attempting to settle with life. When I settled into a career, I never felt fulfilled.

If you fail doing something you love, then you have lived out your life experience doing what you loved. You are better than a compromise. Do not settle for a backup plan. You will never be happy or fulfilled when choosing a backup plan. Experiment with your resources. Jobs are a dime a dozen. You will never be fulfilled or happy if you choose a job that pays you the most money, unless you are passionate about what you are doing. Choose a lifestyle you will want to live and do that for the rest of your life. Upon doing so, you will never work another day in your life again. Be proud of who you are and what you become.

Society defines success as if you are checking off a grocery list of chronological achievements, such as your job title, marriage, neighborhood you live in, car you drive, etc., but it does not define success if you are not *happy*. Earl Nightingale states, "All of us are self-made. Only the successful will admit it." Do not let society dictate what makes you happy. Happiness defines success, nothing else.

CHAPTER SIXTEEN

CONCLUSION

Artificial intelligence is increasing at a rapid rate, to the point where humans will need to adapt as technology continues to evolve. As technology advances, it is more likely that A.I. and machines will replace humans and do the work for them. Jobs have already been replaced by machines, and will not slow down as we head into the future.

Regardless of age, you have seen in your lifetime machines replacing humans on an ongoing basis. For example, when Henry Ford perfected the assembly line, humans were assigned a certain task in order to put the car together. They would switch roles in the factory so the monotony would not drive a person insane. Over time, machines have replaced humans in the monotonous tasks. Companies do this to lower the cost of human labor, which means more money for the company to further advance production in different parts of the world.

Current jobs will become fewer and fewer over time. Today, as a result of advancements in technology, there are fewer cashiers at Walmart or any grocery store due to self-checkout. There are now apps on our phone that can basically disrupt any industry. We have already seen hotel chains become disrupted by short-term rental websites such as Airbnb and VRBO. Taxi drivers have been diluted by Uber and Lyft drivers, which will be soon offset by the entire industry with the advent of driverless cars. Why would Uber or Lyft keep paying for their drivers if they could purchase their own driverless cars and float around from city to city at a much cheaper rate than paying for drivers? The answer is, they would not, and owning cars would be a thing of the past.

As technology continues to evolve, there is not a profession that is safe from being overtaken by A.I. Professions such as lawyers, medics, data entry clerks, chefs, and delivery drivers will soon be taken over by A.I. Does this sound scary to you? Does this mean fewer jobs? The answer is yes and no. There will be fewer jobs that require routine, mundane tasks due to advancements in technology, but new jobs will also be created that have not even been thought of yet. Fewer hours during the workweek can offset the limited jobs that exist today; however, at the same time, we could see a decrease in global population.

Artificial intelligence has become so advanced that the future will take on another life of its own. Advanced civilization and society could evolve to the point where we are looking at alternative living options as global warming continues. Elon Musk is looking to reduce global emissions by utilizing non-pollutant energy as a primary source to fuel the economy. He is also looking to expand civilization outside our atmosphere as a safe haven for involuntarily global destruction.

If we are able to create an environment similar to our living conditions on earth, assuming we cannot turn earth back into earth, then expanding within our galaxy is a future option. Technological advancements, which were unimaginable a few hundred years ago, or even 50 years ago, exist today. As A.I. evolves, it will be able to communicate more effectively with other forms of A.I. Since humans are the programmers, we have the ability to create a being with limited capabilities, but enable its ability to learn from other sources of A.I.

Utilizing the advancements of technology, what if we were able to create a being of some kind and send it to another planet, such as Mars? We could then program all elements for this being. It could become acclimated to the current climate on Mars, ranging from the air it breathes, the weather it is accustomed to, where 70 degrees is considered "hot," minus 80 degrees is normal, and minus 225 is considered cold, to the food it must consume for its "energy" to stay "alive." It will report its findings to earth without the initial risk of living on a foreign planet. While you are sending these beings to Mars, you can place them in different regions of the planet and install a certain belief system, which will simulate and define its culture.

Once you have established its limitations and capabilities, each being different from region to region, you could then make these properties procreate. As this being evolves, you could give it properties to make it think it is making decisions on its own. However, in reality, since you created this being, you are controlling most of its thoughts by sending it messages.

This machine continues to act on its own as it is programmed to do so. The program thinks it is making its own choices from how it is made to think, the tasks it is made to perform, before it becomes taken over by its routine. As you are trying to override the system by sending it thoughts, it continues to be stuck in its routine like it has been infected with a virus, preventing it from breaking control of its habits. As you continue trying to control and manipulate the way it thinks in order for it to become progressive, it becomes so far entrenched in its habits that it will not break free from its pattern.

This form of A.I. will eventually cross paths with a newer version of itself with an entirely different belief system that has been programmed, controlling its way of thinking. This becomes an entirely different form of culture for this program, causing fear of the unknown. It begins to question itself, how something very similar in appearance could think and act differently from itself. As this becomes a threat to the being and its way of life and culture, it attempts to eliminate it. Aggression and war break out, with beings from both "cultures" eventually perishing without ever knowing what they were. What if these beings I am referring to are actually YOU?

When you remove the propaganda that surrounds you, what do you have? The world as you know it has been created by a set of rules, boundaries, and limitations on what we think we can achieve based on our belief system. The world you live in has been constructed and

developed by people no smarter than you. Political borders, boundaries, religion, education, culture, work/play life, habits, etc. have all
been created by other beings. One race, religion, political affiliation,
and culture is not superior to any other affiliation. It is merely a belief system. We are all the same, being programmed on how to think.
When you remove the programs, you will find something that was
lost when it all started. YOUR YOU!

ACKNOWLEDGMENTS

The journey of writing this book taught me that nothing can be accomplished without the entanglement of those you are connected to.

First and foremost, I would like to thank my mother, Jeanne Ashcraft, for being the ultimate supporter during this process. Her first line of review, proofreading, and tirelessly rereading the manuscript during the initial phases, prior to handing it off to an editor, empowered my belief to make this book come into existence.

I am eternally grateful to Amanda Ashcraft for being the angel behind the scenes. Her free spirit, genuine sincerity, and loving support during this journey sparked confidence in me which carried me through the times when I felt lost. Without her, I would not be where I am today.

Thank you to students at Academic Magnet, James Island Charter, School of the Arts, Wando, and West Ashley High School. Every day I get to teach in your school is a gift. You gave me the inspiration I needed to write this book, and I could have not written it without you.

Thank you to my amazing and talented editor, Cassandra Dunn. Her input and feedback helped bring this book to life. It was a joy to work with her and was the smoothest part of the process. Thank you to Taylor Czerwinski for her talented photography skills, website development, straightforward feedback, and especially for being available when I needed her most. Her great vision and ability to adapt enabled me to count on her being a key part to the team.

Thank you to Sunny Dublick for being one of the first to read manuscript, contributing to the foreword and summary, and giving me a sense of feeling that Find Your YOU can be in every household. Thank you to Rose Miller for creating a beautiful book cover design. Thank you to Greg and Natalia of Enchanted Ink Publishing for formatting and being friendly and resourceful when it came to publishing. Thank you Allison Hopper with her timely support and consultation during times that felt uncertain during this journey. Thank you to Chris Carr and Russell Skipper for the encouragement and support at the beginning of writing the manuscript. Thank you to Emily Boykin for being the first to proofread my manuscript. Thank you to Carly Lauer for being available any time I needed her for last minute feedback. Thank you to Yoloha Yoga Studio and all the incredible instructors for teaching me the art of yoga. Their uplifting spirit they bring with them every single day, along with their positivity, encouragement, and energy, helped me get through uncertain times. I am forever grateful to each of them.

I would like to express my love and appreciation to my father, William Ashcraft, twin brother Billy, and older sister, Christine, for always being there whenever I needed them most. Lastly, I would like to extend my warmest gratitude to the friends that became like family: Mike Vigilante and Jonathon Eskie.

SUMMARY

Find Your YOU was created to deliver a message of hope, and provide a path to uncovering the best, most authentic version of yourself. Too often I've talked with students, colleagues, friends, and family members who either couldn't see their purpose, or felt too scared to live it. *Find Your YOU* was created to do just that...to help you let go of the programming, the shame, the guilt – and live a life that is full. One in which you have the ability to be 100% YOU.

We become so busy with life that we forget to live life. *Find Your YOU* will help you discover your authentic self and live your purpose by peeling back the layers of conditioning from your current way of thinking and allowing you to reconnect with who you really are. This book holds the key that separates your YOU from the physical world that is locked away and confined to structure and systemic programming. Once you unlock the door, you will experience a brand new world that you never knew existed.

ABOUT THE AUTHOR

Lifelong educator and author Tony Ashcraft was born in Dearborn, MI. When Tony was twenty-eight, he moved to Charleston, SC, for warmer weather and to gain new experiences in his life. After being primarily a high school teacher for over 10 years, he decided to dabble in the corporate world by joining the financial services industry. After realizing the industry was not for him, he began his journey that led to his ultimate transformation. He devoted the next five years of his life to discovering who he is. He studied the works of past and present New Age thinkers that led to his inward journey. He has found greater peace through his teachings on making the world a better place.

www.tonyaschraft.com

CPSIA information can be obtained
at www.ICGtesting.com
Printed in the USA
LVHW080038310321
683007LV00036B/547

9 781736 421802